BREAKTHROUGH IN GOLF

BUILD A WINNING GOLF SWING
WITH THE HIP TO HIP METHOD™

By
Curtis Elliott

Illustrations by Peter Birren

ISBN: 978-1-4120-4134-8 (sc)

Trafford rev. 06/19/2012

 www.trafford.com

North America & international
toll-free: 1 888 232 4444 (USA & Canada)
phone: 250 383 6864 ♦ fax: 812 355 4082

Dedicated to the memory of my Dad,
Bill Elliott
Who taught me the love of golf

Table of Contents

PREFACE

This it not a regular golf instructional book written by a PGA tour professional. A teaching club pro or long time swing guru has not written it. Instead I am an amateur just like you, (at least until I have published this book for sale). A weekend golfer has written this book. Why would you want to have a weekend golfer try to teach you how to swing a golf club?

While I am not a full time teaching pro, I am a lifelong golfer and an experienced tournament golfer. I currently carry a 2 handicap at my home club, Carolina Golf and Country Club in Charlotte, North Carolina, which was designed by the famed Donald Ross. I am a weekend golfer as a member there. I seldom play more than once a week, although I may sneak in 9 holes on Wednesdays once in a while in the summers.

My PGA teaching background, or lack thereof, however, is not the basis of this book. It is instead my experience of a three-year odyssey of discovery about the golf swing. Like Ben Hogan once said, I firmly believe I have "dug it out of the dirt." As a result of my undertaking a comprehensive study of golf instructional literature, and the focused work I put into my swing over the past three years, I have discovered some very significant things about golf swing fundamentals and more importantly have discovered how to better simplify golf instruction with the method I introduce in this book.

The relationships between cause and effect have revealed swing principles that I never before knew or realized, even though I had spent a lifetime trying to learn how to make my swing work. My study has been highly focused and intensive.

I am a lawyer by profession, and I undertook the study and analysis of the prevailing literature with the same level of preparation and zeal that I would put into preparing a case for trial. Let me take a few minutes to describe it to you. I believe you will better understand why this book may actually help you become a better golfer.

In 2000, my son, Will, was age 11. I started taking him to the driving range to swat a few balls around on the weekends to spend some good quality time with him, and to teach him a little about the game like my Dad did with me. By then my law practice had become a little more established, so I figured that I may as well try to shake the rust off my game to play on the weekends with Will, and try to get a little bit of my game "back." This time, however, I decided to really learn how to swing a club and studiously eliminate any major swing flaws that I might have. I studied many of the major golf instructional books. I also worked on my swing by trial and error and through the use of videotape analysis. I began trying out the swing theories and techniques articulated in the literature.

Working with my own video camera at the driving range and by taking video lessons, I undertook the effort to painstakingly compare and understand what was going in my swing development with the instructional literature I was reading. Not all of what I read squared with what I was seeing on videotape as I improved my swing. I became more keenly interested in analyzing the consistency of instruction in the large body of golf instructional literature and forming my own swing concepts and conclusions. I developed the synthesis and articulation of the swing concepts and methodology in this book as a result of these efforts over the course of several summers.

I believe that through a lot of trial and error and intensive critical analysis, I have stumbled onto an overall swing methodology described in these pages that, if pursued consistently without resort to extraneous gimmicks, actually works to improve a golfer's swing steadily over time. The Hip to Hip Method ™ will not make you a scratch handicapper overnight. But it may very well revolutionize how you go about learning how to swing a golf club, and most importantly of all, it will hopefully simplify your swing thoughts and your ongoing plan of improvement.

There is in a sense not much new with Hip to Hip™. It is primarily based on the principal that a good, solid turn of the hips is essential to a good golf swing. But I believe that the emphasis this book places on the hips combined with a strong **de-emphasis** on the arms, hands, clubshaft and clubhead is new in teaching practice and theory.

The book's focus is on golfers of all levels of ability because the real point of the book rests on rock bottom fundamentals. To use it, you do not have to be a PGA or LPGA tour professional, although I am confident that some players at the top level may also benefit from this book. Those players have day in and day out time to groove any type of swing style under the sun to perfection and make any idiosyncrasies work for them. Fundamentals are even more critical for players who work at full time jobs and are amateur golfers. If you are a typical amateur, you may have an hour or two at most during the week to hit a bucket of balls and keep up your weekend game. So you need something that works within those time constraints.

One final point. I do not hesitate to engage in critical analysis. It is part of my nature as a lawyer to put all issues to the test under the bright light of day. This does not mean that I am one hundred percent right about every issue in this book. I recognize that I am not immune from making my fair share of misjudgments or mistakes. I accept the notion that at least some of the observations I have made in this book may not necessarily hold true for every swing problem of every type of player. I am also sure that more than a few points in this book will likely be debated.

Nonetheless, my goal in these pages is not to win a swing theory debate, but to articulate a broadly relevant swing method, which I have found, through a lot of trial and error, to be a highly successful, simplified swing method that can be readily learned by most golfers and that actually works. I will be pleased to have encouraged further lively discussion and debate among teaching professionals concerning the comparative roles of the hips versus the other moving parts of the golfer's swing. Most importantly, however, I hope that this book will inspire good, productive learning among the millions of golf enthusiasts, young and old, in America and elsewhere.

And I have not only critically analyzed the golf swings of some of history's all time greats, but also carefully parsed some of their instructional words. I found that the words of some of our greats did not and do not always match their actual golf swings. And I found to my surprise that the swing rules enunciated by some of today's leading instructors do not always match what the swing camera shows.

By identifying and highlighting these differences, I mean no disrespect against any of the game's great players or teachers, nor do I mean to unnecessarily create undue controversy about golf swing fundamentals. But in all honesty, the vast body of golf instructional literature simply is not entirely consistent and harmonious. There is simply too much of a hodgepodge of ideas floating around and the average golfer doesn't have the time to filter out what is gimmicky and of fleeting value. Moreover, in my view, golf instructional literature is much too cluttered and complicated. To the extent in this book I have helped harmonize any common understanding of golf swing fundamentals and have helped simplify and accelerate the process of learning, I am honored to have made a contribution to the game.

I cannot resist the temptation to give you a sneak preview on at least one point. I must tell you that in writing this book, I discovered that Bobby Jones had a level of profound understanding of the golf swing that is beyond the understanding of us mere mortals. His astounding words work as well today as they did eighty years ago. The hickory shaft factor, in my view, is a red herring, and instructors of today should be cautioned against discounting Jones's golf swing and his swing ideas as outside the pale of "modern golf" methods. I firmly believe that a trend back toward classic swing theory would be a healthy development in the world of golf instruction. I fervently hope that ardent, lifelong students of the game will agree.

So give the Hip to Hip Method at least a good try, and see whether it works for you. You may surprise yourself. I earnestly hope it will be useful to ongoing generations of golfers of all levels of ability. My son, Will, who is now 18, is using it, and so far, his future prospects as a golfer look bright! I am enjoying getting to play with him more and more as time passes, and look forward to the day he starts beating his dad. I hope your golf swing moves up a notch or two as well. The Hip to Hip Method has definitely moved my golf swing up several notches from the level of skill I had 25 years ago as a member of the men's golf team at the University of South Carolina.

CHAPTER 1

WHY IS SWINGING A GOLF CLUB SO HARD?

Golf is the greatest game of all. It's a game that provides at least a thrill or two every time you play. Whatever your skill level, at least one or two shots a round go right, just as you planned. Of course this occurs along with your fair share of mistakes, bad shots, and if you have a really bad day, sometimes downright misery. But it is a game that can be played throughout your life. You can start at age 4 or 5 and do it over and over again until you are pushing 90, 95 or even 100 if you are still healthy enough to be mobile. And you will never play the same round of golf twice in your whole life. Every round is unique and the shots you hit and the putts you make or miss usually come with their own personality of that day. And, even in the midst of a poor day, all it takes is a couple of good solid shots to keep you coming back for more.

And you can always hope to get better! But can you really? This book is about getting better. We all want to do it. But to get better, we all must understand that learning to swing a golf club is not easy by any stretch of the imagination. This book is about breaking out of the skill rut you find yourself in when swinging the golf club to make a full shot. To begin, we need to grapple with some reality. Consider the following and ask yourself whether any of this sounds familiar.

A TYPICAL DAY IN YOUR LIFE AS A GOLFER

You know the feeling. Finally, it's Thursday afternoon. Your regular foursome at the golf club has a 2 o'clock tee time.

After a hardworking morning at the office, you've decided to eat a quick lunch at the club, take the rest of the afternoon off and have enough time not only to practice putting, but to hit a bucket of balls on the practice range to get your swing going. You're really excited. This time you have time to practice and prepare for your round instead of getting out of the car, running to the locker, slapping on your golf shoes and running out of breath to catch your tee time like you did the last time you played.

Boy, was last week's round bad! You never had the time to practice that low takeaway you had been trying after reading about that new hot tip in the most recent golf magazine. Without time to hit some balls on the range to get your new swing key grooved, you had to think about it as you played out on the course. You shot an 83 that last round, even though you have a 5 handicap. It just didn't feel right when you stood over the ball. The low takeaway idea worked okay for the first seven holes, and you were even par. But the mental focus and swing key feeling soon faded, and you duck hooked that drive on number 8, taking a double bogey.

On the ninth hole, you decided to try your old swing key of pushing the club back with your left hand and nailed your drive 275 yards straight down the middle. But when you tried the old reliable swing key on your 7 iron approach, somehow you felt yourself coming over the top and pulling that 7 iron in the left greenside sand trap. After blasting out, you three putted. Another double. Okay, so you were four over on the front nine.

On the tenth tee, you went back to the low takeaway and bingo! It worked beautifully! You birdied number 10 to go 3 over. From that point on, your swing disintegrated. You played the last 8 holes in bogey golf. Eleven over for the day! If you would have only had time to practice that low takeway on the driving range before the round! Maybe next time it will be better, you thought.

And today it will be better! You have close to an hour after lunch to hit range balls so you can't wait to play today. You get to the range, do a few stretches, hit a few wedges and pull out your 5 iron. "Okay" you say to yourself, "let's work on that low takeaway!" So you hit the first 5 iron, sweeping the club along the ground. You flush the shot, dead in the middle of the clubface, and the ball flys straight down the range as if on a clothesline. You address the next ball, thinking "low and slow". A little thin, but the ball flys straight. And another. And another. And another. They all are flying straight! The low takeaway feels a little uncomfortable but you keep at it. The ball is making flush contact with the clubhead.

You hit 9 out of 10 five irons almost dead perfect and straight at the practice range pin 170 yards out! Now you pull out a 3 iron. Same result. Low and slow, drag the clubhead, sweep the grass. The swing thoughts seem to be working. Five good shots in a row. The sixth shot is a hook, but you somehow felt your hands "slapping at" the ball halfway down your downswing. Maybe you should hit a few shots in slow motion to smooth out your tempo. That's it! Low, slow and slow coming down! Low, slow and slow coming down! You hit 5 of 7 of the next 3 irons flush, and the adrenaline begins to flow. Maybe you've got the groove this afternoon, finally!

You pull out the driver. Low, slow and slow coming down. Low, slow and slow coming down. You drill 5 straight drives dead in the middle of the clubface with your new titanium driver! This low, slow and slow coming down thinking is really working! The way you're nailing it, a 73 or 74 will be on your scorecard by the end of the afternoon!

At that, you're off to the putting green and after 10 or 15 minutes making a few and missing a few, you're on the first tee. Your partner saw you hitting balls on the range and remarks to the others to ask for shots from you today because you looked like a machine on the range. You peg up your ball on the first tee, pick your spot in the fairway to target, take a deep breath, think "low, slow and slow coming down" and the next thing you see is your drive screaming down the middle, landing 290 yards out, leaving you a 9 iron to the green.

When you get to your ball in the first fairway, you take out the 9 iron, think low, slow and slow coming down, and hit a smooth feeling shot that falls like a feather on top of the pin. Walking up to the green, you feel so confident, knowing a great round is in the works. You walk up to repair your ball mark, and calmly roll in your three footer for birdie. What a great start! On the second hole, you do it again, this time hitting a long drive and a 6 iron to ten feet, and you make it! Two under for the first two holes! Low and slow, slow coming down.

And so it goes, shot after shot after shot. You make the turn 1 under. Okay so you had a three putt on number 5, but your low and slow, slow on the way down has done nothing but put your full swing on a string. It all seems so easy. How can you hit 8 of 9 greens on the front without even trying? This is what golf is all about! All those balls hit on the range over the summer, all the practice putting, all those lessons, all those golf instructional books read. It's now all paying off!

And it keeps on going! Through 16 you are 2 under, picking up another birdie on 14. Standing on the 17th tee, you begin to think about breaking 70. Number 17 is a short par four, with a speed slot down the left side, but the fairway slopes left into a heavily wooded area. No use trying to hit it hard, just a smooth swing down the left side. Low, slow and slow coming down. Okay, you draw the clubhead back. It seems in slow motion. Slow, but hey! Half way back on your backswing you wondered why in the world did you "feel" your hands pick up the clubhead, and ugh! What happened? The downswing feels like a lunge! Oh no! The ball snaps sharply to the left. As you watch the ball dart into the left woods, you're thinking to yourself, "why did I pick the clubhead up and jerk it during the downswing?"

After looking for your drive for what seems to be an eternity, you finally declare it lost, go back to the tee box with a penalty shot, and hit another swooping hook into the woods. Two lost drives! Hitting five off the tee you wander down the fairway in shock, and somehow scrape a wedge onto the green. You hardly notice the 10 footer you make from 12 feet for a triple bogey 7. Another duck hook drive on the 18th results in a double bogey on the last hole. Three over par, a 74. Okay so you shot one shot below your handicap today. But what a wasted opportunity! You have never broken 70 at your club, and this was your big chance. Who knows when the next time will be?

But in the locker room, you can't get over how good you played the first 16 holes and how quickly your swing evaporated on the last two holes when the pressure was on. You hate this game! No, not really. You love this game, but it can be so frustrating. You say to yourself, "I can't wait to try that swing out next week. Maybe if I take the club a little more to the outside, I can eliminate that hook." You think on and off all the next week about hitting balls and taking the clubhead back outside. For once and all you will eliminate that hook shot when the pressure is on! Just a few sessions taking the clubhead back a little outside and it will all fall into place.

Does this whole up and down scenario sound typical? For too many golfers of all levels of ability, this pattern of practice, play and swing key thought and swing key thought changes is all too common. Your perfect swing is just around the corner, but somehow it never "kicks in." Why is your golf swing so inconsistent, so ephemeral, and so fleeting? One day the magic is there. The next day it's gone. Nothing seems to permanently hang together with your golf swing. We all wonder why it is so hard to consistently swing a golf club halfway effectively.

THE QUEST TO BE BETTER

Anyone who plays golf regularly wants to improve. The last pure shot we hit always brings us back. Every golfer strives for that one key swing thought or swing feel, or swing tempo that will bring him or her closer to the universal goal of swing improvement. But how should a golfer seek to improve? At the professional level on the PGA and LPGA Tours, it is widespread practice to hire a swing guru or coach, hit balls every day, analyze hours of video footage and confer at length with the coach on all aspects of swing technique, set up, timing, tempo and the like.

At this level slavish adherence to universally orthodox golf swing fundamentals is probably less important due to the amount of time a successful touring pro has to devote to ironing out a repeating golf swing. A very good example of one of the pros who possess a beautifully consistent swing that works, and works under world class pressure is Jim Furyk, winner of the 2003 U.S. Open. Although his looping, ultra high plane swing is highly personal, unorthodox and unique to him, he knows his own habits.

Furyk works continuously to keep his groove, and is comfortable with what works very well for him. His comfort with his own personal mechanics and his wonderful sense of tempo and timing prove that the real secret to a sound golf swing is simply building and maintaining one that you can confidently repeat. If the golf swing repeats good and excellent golf shots, everything else is, in the end, totally irrelevant.

But aside from the touring professional or aspiring near professionals like national level collegiate golfers (and today high school or lower grades), most golfers find themselves either in the work a day world or retired, and unwilling to have golf consume their lives. The amateur, casual or serious, 90-shooter or scratch handicapper, simply does not have the time or inclination to focus so intensely on finely grinding down a world class golf swing on a daily basis.

So the "part timer" is left with a little practice range time and hopes that periodic personal instruction from the local swing coach or teaching pro or reading lots of golf instructional books or magazine tips will yield some good results. But where do you start and how do you proceed? What is the best way to improve your ball striking ability and swing consistency within your limited time budget? And what are some of the obstacles to overcome to arrive at the point of solid improvement and consistent results?

OBSTACLES TO GOLF SWING IMPROVEMENT

Why is it so hard to learn how to swing a golf club well, or at any level of expertise, swing the club better and better? Even top amateurs and professionals struggle with the almost impossible goal of steadily improving the day-to-day performance that goes with hitting a golf ball. There are numerous obstacles to making solid progress with your golf game and, in particular, with your golf swing. A sampling follows.

Golf Swing Complexity

In addition to the time constraints conspiring against non-touring pro golfers to keep their own personal "groove" like Jim Furyck, there is the problem of complexity. The problem is not just limited to the complexity of athletic movement involved in both a well-done golf swing and a poor golf swing. In a golf swing, the athletic movement itself is incredibly sophisticated. Getting a shot just right is probably one of the most demanding tasks in all of sports, at least in terms of the intricacy and precision required to physically pull off all of the movements all at once.

The other dimension of the complexity problem is the sheer complexity of golf swing theory, swing ideas, previously published golf swing knowledge and instructional technique, educational material, drills, video recordings, golf school experiences, variance of opinions, and practice tee instructional approaches to understanding and learning how to swing a golf club. By all appearances, the swing itself has so many moving parts that occur within the 1 to 1.8 seconds it takes to swing a club from start to finish, it is a wonder how the clubhead ever even makes its way back to the ball for anything close to solid contact.

Think about it. To deliver a clubhead consistently into the back of a golf ball at the right angle with the face geometrically correct and facing down the target line with a solid, descending blow into the back of the ball, your center of gravity holding the centrifugal force of the swing radius together has to be standing at the exact same distance from the ball at impact as you were at address. You must be aligned properly at address with feet, hips, shoulders, arms and clubface parallel to the ball flight line. You must have gripped the club in a manner that insures the clubface will square up at impact precisely while traveling 100 to 130 miles per hour starting from above your head. You must have taken the club back on a swing path with hands, arms, shoulders and hips on a line and angle, and at a speed, tempo and synchronization that not only minimizes compensating adjustments coming back down, but builds enough leverage, full body coil and wrist cock capable of generating power, speed and precision all at the same time.

Trying to execute such an extremely involved and intricate set of athletic moves in a second and a half, much less attempting to think about any of it at all, is almost like pulling all the human tasks, mechanical actions, computer calculations, logistics scheduling, and power generation moves NASA makes during the entire week period of a manned spacecraft flight to the moon! On top of the actual athletic act of swinging a golf club, you are tempted to consider a vast body of knowledge and thought to incorporate into your swing, either in the act consciously or subconsciously at a driving range, or in the confines of your garage or living room at home as you contemplate how to swing a golf club.

Hundreds of thousands of pages of golf theory and instruction breaking down the golf swing into the minutest detail of every centimeter of movement have been published over the last one hundred years.

Lack of Muscle Flexibility

Another key impediment to making good golf swings is muscle flexibility, or rather the lack of it. Many modern golf instructional sources stress how important "coil" is during the backswing. The idea of "coil" is that a golfer's shoulders and arms will wind up over his hips so that like a loaded spring, the player is wound up for a powerful release of built up tension during the downswing to generate power and forceful clubhead path.

The problem many golfers have with the concept of coil, especially older golfers, is that a full turn is simply not physically possible. All the pros on tour have enormous shoulder turns and backswing windup. It looks great and seems so easy watching on TV, but the reality is that level of flexibility must be achieved either by hitting lots of balls every day or doing something to stretch out the muscles to enable that type of turn on the backswing. Any attempt to generate power by other means, particularly with the hands and arms as a substitute for a full wide backswing turn, will result in artificial clubhead movement going back, which in turn compels compensating adjustments coming back through. These adjustments are not reliable, because so many of them are dependent upon tempo and timing being perfect on that day.

Additionally, as this book will show, the concept of coil by creating backswing resistance of the hips is a myth. At least coil in the sense of turning the shoulders 90 degrees during the backswing while limiting the turn of the hips is a myth, and it violates simple physics. This book will show that the degree to which the shoulders turn is tied to, and in fact, almost totally dependent upon the degree to which the hips turn during the swing. Simply put, no full hip turn, no full shoulder turn. Coil in the sense that tension will naturally build up as a consequence of a full turn of the shoulders as a result of A FULL TURN OF THE HIPS is a valuable and workable swing ideal. Coil in the sense of creating tension by restricting the backswing hip turn is artificial, physically impossible to achieve and seriously damaging to the player's ability to focus on much more meaningful swing goals.

Part of this book is devoted to describing some isometric exercises and stretches that have worked very effectively for me in building the muscle flexibility and stretch needed to make a supple but smooth move during the backswing and the downswing. These stretching techniques will build far more coil than you can ever achieve by artificially trying to restrict the hip turn during the backswing while turning the shoulders.

Swing Tips and Fads

Probably one of the biggest obstacles to learning how to build a good golf swing is the vast magnitude of instructional materials available to you. There is a huge body of hot swing fads, swing tips, novelty drills, pithy suggestions, corny band-aid ideas and faulty fundamentals in today's golf literature. The typical bookstore has dozens of golf instructional books by various authors, each of whom have a different take on what makes a good golf swing. The better books do demonstrate a certain level of convergence about the swing fundamentals common to great ball strikers. The consensus that exists among the top books by the top instructors do give comfort to the student who is ardent in studying all of them and diligent in developing a synthesis of understanding about the fundamentals.

For example, Ben Hogan's "*Five Lessons, The Modern Fundamentals of Golf*" is widely acknowledged as articulating some of the most sound golf swing fundamentals ever written. Hogan's analysis of the set up, the grip, the takeaway, the backswing, swing plane, the transition to the downswing and the downswing endure today as statements of swing fundamentals that most top teachers recognize as gospel truth. The devil is in the details, however, and figuring out how to master those fundamentals through muscle memory development can be a tremendous task that takes years of hard thought and practice to accomplish.

An even greater obstacle to learning is the flood of fads and hot tips that golf magazines put out on a weekly or monthly basis. To the non-expert golfer, these fads and hot tips can actually prevent any real golf swing improvement. Why? The non-expert golfer who has not acquired enough discernment as to what is sound fundamental teaching and what is a useless gimmick can be easily overwhelmed with the hodgepodge. After all there are 10 to 20 swing tips and gimmicks a month in most golf magazines. Which one will bring on the quick fix? Why not try them all? If none of the month's quick fixes work, just wait for the next month's edition and pick up 10 to 20 more "great" ideas. For golfers starving to gain some level of skill and understanding, this is like popping pills. A new quick fix for every day of the week! Maybe the next one will work! The magic solution!

Have you ever wondered why there are so many fads and tips offered each month by the golf magazines? Golf instruction, like sex, sells! Getting the latest and greatest instructional tips is a lot of the reason why many golfers buy golf periodical magazines. So the more ideas the better, no matter how disconnected or marginal many of the ideas turn out to be. It seems like every club professional who is featured in one of the tips pages has to have a pithy, unique idea that nobody else has ever thought of, that pro's unique brand of an idea. But unfortunately, these quilt like patchworks of hot fads and tips featured in the monthly periodicals have no unifying theme, and are seldom, if ever, subjected to critical analysis by top peer instructors.

The Real Problem with Tips and Secrets

The above illustrations show that many of the so-called tips and secrets, when subject to analysis against the backdrop of commonly accepted swing fundamentals, simply hold no water. Moreover, these tips can actually impair or even undermine a golfer's efforts to develop sound swing fundamentals. Obviously, this is not true of all tips and secrets. Some magazine tips are extremely sound fundamentally and can greatly accelerate swing development, subject to a big "if". The if is that the golfer reader understands a great swing idea when he or she sees it and can distinguish between a tip that just a poorly grounded tip (compared to widely accepted fundamentals) and a "tip" that has some real value grounded in basic fundamentals.

The real problem with tips and secrets, however, is the band-aid effect. Quick swing cures simply lack any unified concept of how the golf swing works. A unified concept of the golf swing is needed as a guidepost or a set of measurement standards for what the real goal of thinking how to swing is. The real goal in thinking about golf swing instruction is to learn how to assess whether what the player is actually doing is moving his or her swing in the right direction. Golf swing instruction should focus less on detailed mid-swing (or pre-swing, or post-swing) mechanical technique and more on what the swing is trying to accomplish. What is the goal of the golf swing and how can a player work toward the goal by making refinements in his or her swing pattern?

THE CURSE OF HANDS AND ARMS

Another huge obstacle to learning how to swing a golf club is, in my view, a heavily misplaced instructional focus on the hands and arms as key swing factors. As the following chapters of this book will explain, I believe that the movement of the hands and arms during the golf swing are, from an instructional standpoint, almost totally irrelevant. This may strike some golfers, and instructors, as strange. After all, don't the hands hold on to the club during the swing, and isn't the swing in large part the unleashing of the club shaft by the arms through impact? How about wrist cock and release? Don't strong forearms make any difference? How about all of the talk about how well a player uses his or her "hands" during the golf swing?

Of course the hands and arms are integral parts of the golf swing. Any movie of a golf swing or frame by frame swing analysis clearly shows the hands and the arms swinging the club back to the top, cocking the wrists as the backswing finishes, and forcefully lashing through the ball at impact in a strong intense manner. But are we looking at cause or effect?

How can the arms be left out of the swing? The clearly obvious answer is that from a purely physical they cannot. The swinging motion of the arms is from a strictly visual perspective, the front and center stage of what we see when we watch someone make a golf swing. And visual observations aside, the whiplash effect created by a strong arm swing and cocking and uncocking of the wrists during the swing is a critical and essential component in generating power and delivering it into the clubhead as it passes into the back of a golf ball within the impact zone. But, as I will demonstrate over the rest of this book, the importance of mentally focusing on the muscular movement of the hands and arms during the golf swing, as points of instructional reference, has very little instructional value.

Do I mean that the arms and hands have no role during the golf swing? No. The hands and arms, after all, are connected to the golf club and are vital in the transmission of the clubhead in a powerful manner into the back of the golf ball. But do the hands and arms have any vital role to play in the player's initiation or execution of the golf swing as a conscious, mental athletic act? In my view, they do not. Your hands and arms need not be cut off to improve your golf swing, but I am saying that the muscular movement of the hands and arms for most part of the golf swing can be virtually passive in a great golf swing, and in many great golf swings are indeed passive. Using the hands, arms clubshaft or clubhead as points of reference in building a golf swing is not only fruitless, it is, in my view, seriously counterproductive.

In my estimation the visual appearance of someone swinging a golf club is misleading, for it artificially compels the observer to conclude that the arms are where the action is. The fallacy, however, is that looks in this critical area are indeed deceiving. It is the hips, torso and shoulders turning and unwinding that indeed drive the arms and hands. And the unwinding of the hips, torso and shoulders does more than generate power. In the golf swing of expert players, the unwinding of the hips, torso and shoulders actually controls the swing path of the clubshaft and clubhead by pulling the arms and hands along the arc which will square the clubhead into the back of the ball, down the target line. This is a fundamental corollary to the principle that the large body swing fulcrums—the hips, torso and shoulders—should drive and dominate the swing.

The Instructional Problem:
Thinking About the Hands and Arms

The problem with the arms and hands lies not really in their use, but in the conscious attention given to them in instructional material and in actual attempts by golfers in making a golf swing. The focus on hands and arms, and indirectly the hand and arms by instructionally focusing on the clubhead, the takeaway path, or the cocking of wrists is a harmful impediment to golf swing learning in two key respects. First, these swing ideas, whether expressed as swing theories, methods, or "hot tips", divert your attention away from focusing on the target or the movement of the large moving parts of the swing. As this book will show, your larger muscles of your hips and shoulders can much more effectively be used to control the swing. These muscles will not only act more effectively as swing power generators, but more importantly as swing pathway governors, from the standpoint of learning and swing key management during play.

Second, focusing mental attention to movements of the hands, arms and clubhead invokes an unreasonable matrix of mechanical complexity. That prevents you from focusing on one or two simple thoughts, such as the shot target and a simple body movement during the 1.5 seconds of a full swing. There simply is not enough time to consciously think about mechanical details that are so heavily dependent on sheer timing.

For example, there is a ton of golf instruction that focuses on "taking the clubhead back straight," or taking the clubhead back "low and slow." The idea is that if you "take" the clubhead straight back from the ball, and particularly if the clubhead moves away from the ball "low and slow" then not only will good tempo be created, but the proper swing path for the arms, clubhead, arms, shoulders and swing plane will result. A mental focus on taking the clubhead straight back from the ball causes the focal point of movement to be the hands and arms, since they are connected to the club. But the idea can easily lead to artificial manipulation because, in a great golf swing, the clubhead does not move straight back from the ball for more than a very few inches.

After a couple of inches, the clubhead in an excellent swing, without any further manipulation of the hands or wrists due to early wrist cock, will swiftly begin moving to the inside of the target line because the arc of the clubhead swing, due to the rotation of the player's hips and shoulders, revolves around the hub of the swing in a circular fashion. What is the hub of the swing? It is at a point on the golfer's spine somewhere between the top of the hipbones and the bottom of the golfer's shoulder blades.

An excellent mental picture that can help you conceptually understand the hub of your golf swing is that point on you spine, which is about even with your belly button. The whole golf swing revolves around this hub, and its center of gravity and centrifugal force resides there. That is why the clubhead begins to quickly swing inside the target line after a few inches. That is also why trying to force the clubhead back too straight from the ball at takeaway pulls the clubshaft off the circular arc pathway and off the balance of gravity at the hub. This can in turn destroy your balance and even cause the arms to artificially lift the clubhead up in a steep angle during the backswing instead of swinging the club back in a winding motion when done correctly.

Causing the Actual Problem:
Overuse of Arms and Hands

Thinking about moving the clubhead, the hands or the arms in a particular manner as focal points of swinging a golf club can obviously lead to overemphasis of the actual use of the hands and arms during the swing. Even if these key thoughts are not used to drive the swing, the player can be guilty of making poor swings by actually overusing the hands and arms during the swing. Well, okay you may be thinking, this all sounds good, but what's so bad about the hands and arms? The breakdown in your golf swing resulting from overuse of the hand and arms will usually cause one of two bad results, depending on whether you are a high or medium handicapper, or a low handicapper. The negative consequences, however, are equally severe. The good news is that the bad outcomes of overusing the hands and arms are uniquely tied to the overuse and are entirely predictable.

Over the Top With Arms:
The High Handicapper's Curse

If you are a high handicapper what happens if you overuse your hands or arms? It will generally depend on your balance. Let's take a look at what happens when the arms get into the act too much.

If you lack the ability to fully turn your body on the backswing and coil properly the backswing movement dominated by the hands and arms usually cause the clubhead to be picked up in too steep an angle. At the top of the backswing, the right hand takes over, and casts the clubhead toward the ball in a heave ho manner similar to a lumberjack chopping wood. High handicappers tend to initiate their downswings with their hands instead of their hips. If that happens, several bad things can, and will happen, depending on which errors multiply which other errors:

1. If your downswing fails to get your weight shifted to your left foot, and the hands attack the ball at the start of the downswing, the entire swing plane of the clubshaft is thrown over the top of the correct swing path. In other words, the clubhead is swung "outside in." The clubhead, as it enters the impact zone with the uncocking of the wrists is delivered into the ball from the outside, with the clubface usually facing down the line or worse, to the right of the target line. This causes the ball to be banana sliced severely off to the right. The problem can even be worsened if you suffer from "reverse weight shift" which is the loading up during the backswing of weight on the left foot that then shifts back to the right foot during the downswing causing an exacerbated over the top motion.

2. If you don't shift your balance off of your right foot during the downswing, but you somehow are able to manipulate your hands in a manner that closes up the clubface, your over the top downswing will still deliver the clubhead from outside in, but you may only actually pull the ball somewhat or severely to the left of the target with a pulled shot, because the clubface squared up enough to avoid slice sidespin on the ball.

3. If you somehow fail to shift your weight back to your left foot during the downswing, but also commit the sin most

low handicappers commit with their hands, by rolling the wrists over at impact, you can actually hit a severe pull hook. A pull hook is caused when the clubhead is delivered from outside the target line and at the moment of impact, the wrists roll over severely, overshooting the clubface so that it is actually facing left of the clubhead line of delivery. If the clubhead's actual line of delivery is outside in and the clubface is closed to the clubhead path, then it is severely closed compared to the target line, and it imparts hook sidespin onto the ball.

The basic problem with all of the above bad outcomes is that the clubhead is delivered from outside the target line into the ball as you swing over the top. Eliminating the over the top movement of the arms at the beginning of the golf swing is one of the toughest swing flaws to overcome by high handicappers, but as this book will show, it can be done with some good drills to get the hips into the act with the leading role they deserve.

Rolling Wrists:
The Curse of Low Handicap Players

If you are a low handicapper or a pretty good player who can regularly shoot in the seventies or eighties, you are much less likely to have the balance problems of the high handicapper. You probably have somewhat of a decent turn of your shoulders going back, and are able to make the transition from backswing to downswing by moving your weight back to your left foot. But you find that timing matters so much. If you get "too quick" with your hands, you tend to hit a bad hook, or if you slide your hips or upper body too much forward during the downswing you can be prone to blocking the shot out to the right. For a good part of the time, how well you strike the golf ball on any given day all depends on your timing. If you have good tempo on a given day, the occasional bad push or hook can be kept to a minimum and on really good days these bad shots may not even show up during the round. But on a pressure shot down the stretch, or on a bad tempo day, you are fighting to keep the ball in the fairway and find yourself trying to get up and down from way too many missed greens.

What is often happening in these cases is a bad case of rolling wrists. Your backswing gets the swing plane of your clubshaft pretty well set at the top but at the beginning of the downswing, it begins to fall apart. If you shift your weight quickly back onto your left side, but fail to make an aggressive unwinding of the hips, your hands tend to drop into the inside of the target line sometimes a little too much and if the clubface does not square up quick enough, then a large push of the shot to the right will occur.

If instead your hands "overcook" in an attempt to square up the clubface, your forearms and in particular your wrists may begin to roll over, with the right hand and wrist rolling over the top of the left wrist and hand as a means to square up the clubface. If your timing is perfect, the clubface will not flip closed to the target line too quickly and you can find yourself pulling the shot off. But if your wrists roll over too soon, the clubface shuts down to a closed position as the clubhead moves into the back of the ball, causing either a slight draw or hook, a sweeping hook or a sharp duck hook. Using the wrists and hands to square up the clubface at impact rather than a rapid spinning or clearing of the hips at impact places entirely too much reliance on impeccable timing.

Okay, so if the heart of the problem with golfers of all levels is the overactive use of arms and hand during the swing, what is the heart of the solution? Does overcoming the swing flaws tied to overused hands and arms take years of ball hitting on the driving range to overcome? I submit that the answer is no, provided the golfer has a fundamental understanding of what makes for a very good golf swing, and can then formulate a strategy how to move in the right direction.

CHAPTER 2

HIP TO HIP ™:
A UNIFIED SWING THEORY

If the central problem with a bad golf swing is the misuse of the hands and arms, then as a matter of golf swing instruction, and as a part of the athletic action of trying to consciously make a decent golf swing, what is the central solution to it all? The answer I submit can become clear when the swing action of top golfers is compared to the swing action of lesser skilled golfers. Another way to get to the bottom of the instructional morass is to examine the golf instructional statements about swing fundamentals made by the top world class players in history. When their comments are fully analyzed in detail and stacked up against what other great players in history say, and what other instructional sources have to offer, we can begin to see the points of departure in golf swing theory and question those fissures.

THE REAL DIFFERENCE BETWEEN EXPERTS AND NOVICES: HIP DOMINATION.

What All Great Ball Strikers Have in Common

Let's forget swing mechanics for a few moments. Let's forget all the instruction of the past 100 years. Let's even forget that the golf swing is a dynamic athletic action. Let's forget for a moment that there is even such a thing as golf swing. Let's simply look at some basic facts of geometry. What is the geometry of a great golf swing at the moment of truth, at impact? And what is the geometry of a poor golf swing at the moment of truth? How do these two compare?

There are many types of styles and methods of golf swings and just as there are many types of players, golf swings come in all sizes and shapes. At the critical moment of truth however, all great golf swings look surprisingly alike, and all great golf swings look different from poor swings in only one overall respect. It is THE master key fundamental to proper impact between the golf clubhead and the golf ball and the ONE key swing goal that all players should strive for. It is the relationship between the arms and hips at impact.

Expert Impact Hip Angle: Open Hips

From front or back, let's look down the target line at the impact point in the swing of a golfer with an excellent swing. What does it always show? It shows that while the arms and shoulders are parallel to the target line at impact, the hips are not. The hips are opened significantly more, and are facing well left of the target line in the case of a right-handed player. In other words, the player's hips have turned more back through AND PAST the target line than the player's shoulders and arms, sometimes 45 degrees or more from the hip line parallel to the ball's target line. Thus, the ultimate critical fact of geometry in a golf swing is that the hips have spun out of the way, or "cleared" way beyond "parallel" to the target line of the ball in order to pull the clubhead around enough to square up at impact. A novice player's hips are at an angle open to the target line by 20 to 30 degrees at the moment the ball is struck. Most top PGA or LPGA touring pros have opened their hips closer to 45 degrees from the target line at impact.

The most compelling factor in a sound, well struck shot is this: IN A FULL POWERFUL SWING, WHEREBY THE CLUBHEAD IS DELIVERED FROM INSIDE THE TARGET LINE (AS OPPOSED

TO FROM OUTSIDE THE TARGET LINE WHICH WILL MOST LIKELY GENERATE A SEVERE SLICE) THE ONLY TECHNIQUE THAT CONSISTENTLY SQUARES UP THE CLUBFACE AT IMPACT IS TO HAVE THE HIPS SPUN WELL PAST THE BALL'S TARGET LINE AS THE ARMS AND SHOULDERS ARRIVE AT IMPACT. THERE IS NO OTHER RELIABLE METHOD OR SECRET TO SQUARING UP THE CLUBFACE. Assuming that the clubhead is delivered from inside the target line, down the correct plane line, no other technique or method works as a mechanical matter.

While it is true that a straight golf shot can be hit if the hips have not spun past the target line if the hands miraculously time the release of the wrists out or the wrists roll the clubface shut, these are highly unpredictable, and extremely inconsistent timing solutions that are simply not reliable. The only swing mechanic that works is open hips at impact, and it is the only swing mechanic that "guarantees" good timing at impact.

You can easily prove the point to yourself with a little experiment. Refer to Illustration 2.1. Standing as if you were addressing a shot, do not move your body, but swing your right arm back in a totally relaxed manner back and forth along the impact zone. How square does the palm or your right hand stay to the target line? Not much. Watch how the palm of your right hand, much like a clubface held in your right hand if your were actually swinging a golf club, rolls over and shuts closed just when it gets to your left heel, where the ball normally is placed on a full shot. Now, turn your hips open so that all of your weight is on your left foot, and your belt buckle is facing down the target line. Ilustration 2.2 shows that as you swing your right arm back and forth along the impact zone, watch what the palm of your right hand does. THE RIGHT HAND NEVER ROLLS! The palm of your right hand simply faces down the target line without any rollover or twisting. Don't you think you could hit more consistent golf shots if your hands were not twisting or rolling at impact?

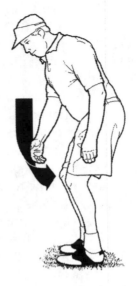

Ill. 2.1—Closed hips cause the hands to "rollover" at impact as the arms swing past the body.

Ill. 2.2—Open hips prevent "rollover" at impact as the arms swing past the body.

The open hips at impact fundamental further means that from an instructional point of view, and movement of the golf swing leading up to impact must either incorporate the goal of open hips at impact or be flawed as a swing teaching technique as a matter of sound golf swing fundamentals. No ifs ands or buts. A teacher may well point out that some golfers may be physically inhibited from clearing the hips open at impact. Allowing for exceptions on this point completely misses the point of the most compelling fundamental of an excellent golf swing. THE ESSENCE OF A FUNDAMENTALLY SOUND GOLF SWING IS OPEN HIPS AT IMPACT.

Now, it is true that other fundamental components of the swing must be working for a good shot to occur, because balance must be there, the proper weight transfer must be there, a good swing plane must be there, the player's head must be relatively steady, and the player must stay down and through the shot. But assuming that the clubhead is being delivered into the back of the ball, the open hips factor must exist to square up the clubface in a consistent manner.

Hip Angles of Beginners, Novices and Poorly Swinging Experts

In contrast to swings that are in the category of excellent with the open hip at impact as a key feature, there are swings lacking in this most fundamentally important characteristic. The lack of good strong, vigorous unwinding of the left hip at impact that has rotated well past the target line can occur in the swings of both high and low handicappers.

In the case of a low handicapper, the lack of full left hip rotation through impact is usually accompanied by a lack of hip windup during the backswing, as well as a lack of strong dynamic balance through the downswing. As discussed more fully in the following chapters, the golfer's balance shifts back to and loads up onto the right foot during the backswing and then moves back to the left foot at the beginning of the downswing as the left hip starts its turn back toward the target. However, the weight shift back and then forward is not a lateral movement of the player's hips or upper body. Instead, the shift in weight is very closely tied to the turn of the hips back and forth throughout the swing.

Proper weight shift fundamentally depends upon a correct wind and unwind of the hips. The golfer's entire swing is a circular, inclined "flywheel" that is propelling the clubshaft around a circular center of gravity with intense centrifugal force and unless the player's center of gravity is anchored during the entire swing, the arc of the clubhead swing path with be destroyed. Only if the hips move correctly can correct dynamic balance be maintained.

A key flaw often seen in poor golf swings void of correct weight shift is a collapse at impact of the left arm and wrist. This is also frequently accompanied by an over and out hijacking of the swing by the golfer's right arm and hand at the beginning of the downswing. The high handicapper does not have strong hip turn through impact so the only way the player can return the clubhead anywhere close to the ball is by casting the clubhead at it with a huge slap of the right hand and wrist. The result is that the clubhead is almost "thrown" at the ball as the left arm breaks down and the left wrist cups at impact. If the player is lucky enough to have timed the unleashing of the clubshaft just perfectly, the clubhead will miraculously square up and deliver into the back of the ball for a solid shot. This may result in a solid shot but does not guarantee a straight shot because if the club is not delivered from inside the target line but from outside the line (a flaw that again is usually tied to leaving weight on the right foot during the downswing) then a big slice will occur.

Good players can also suffer from a lack of strong hip rotation at impact. Low handicappers and professionals usually have good full shoulder turns during the backswing so that the arms are not grossly picked up or abruptly lifted during the backswing and as a result have a good swing plane going at the top of the backswing that enables delivery of the clubhead during the downswing from inside the target line.

Bad slicing is usually not a problem with low handicappers unless there is some problem with the grip in relation to the clubface at impact. But another problem can occur, and often does occur with both low handicappers and top touring professional. The problem goes as follows. The very good player, who usually has a good full shoulder turn, takes the club back on a good wide arc and makes a good full shoulder turn going back, while loading his or her weight onto the right foot at the top of the backswing. But next, as the transition of the downswing by a shift of weight toward the left foot occurs, the player fails to make an aggressive rotation of hips counterclockwise and left past the target line, and instead "slides" the hips forward.

A common visual marker reflecting an improper slide of the hips instead of a brisk unwinding of the hips is the bent left knee at impact. Great players like Tiger Woods "post up" or straighten the left leg at impact as the left hip spins around the left foot and clears past the target line. In contrast, a bent left knee shows that it is absorbing the downswing force of the swing and allowing the swing's circular center to shift toward the target, which in turn forces the clubhead to stay inside the target line too long. If no compensations are made during the downswing, the clubhead will be delivered into the inside back of the ball in an inside out swing path, causing a push of the shot to the right.

But what if compensations occur? Good players have the ability to make compensations during the downswing, although they are often unconsciously made. The clubhead and clubshaft gets too much inside the target line at the top of the backswing, and drops further inside the line as the player's right elbow drives back into his or her right side. At this point, real trouble starts. Somehow "sensing" that the left hip is sliding toward the target and not rotating past it, the player subconsciously "feels" that the clubhead is not about to square up and to avoid a big right push or "block out" the wrists get into the action, the right wrist begins to do the work the turning hips should have done by squaring up the clubface with a rolling action whereby the right hand "turns over" the left hand as the club approaches the impact zone.

If the player's timing is impeccable, everything works out fine, the clubface squares, and the shot is pulled off. But if the hands "turn over" too quickly, the clubface shuts down as it enters impact, causing a push hook or swooping hook if the player's hips and upper body get too far in front of the ball, or a bad left hook, if they do not. Good players who are suffering hooking problems are often overhead complaining about "getting too quick" or "swing too hard at it." Often, however, the reality of the problem is that the hands and wrists were forced to do the job meant for the hips. The hips at impact not the hands must square the clubhead.

The Case for Hips From Start to Finish: Eliminating Complexity

A golf swing based on an outstanding winding and unwinding of the hips eliminates the role of timing as the key determinant of whether a good or poor shot results because the clubface is squared up with a very rapid and brisk rotation of the torso. Moreover, a hip dominated swing eliminates entire libraries of swing thought from the player's mind because it guides all of the movements of the rest of the player's moving parts, the shoulders, and the arms and hands. How does this work?

In a swing not dominated by the hips, everything concerning swing mechanics gets very complicated. During the takeaway, a player whose swing is not hip driven is worried about "taking it back straight", taking it "back slow", or keeping his or her weight on the inside of the right foot, coming up with a swing "trigger" that will initiate a smooth takeaway, making a full shoulder turn, cocking the wrists at the right moment, and other assorted arm, hand and shoulder variations to get it all together.

In a hip dominated swing, the player's focus is winding up the right hip in the proper fashion, which in turn takes all of the jerkiness out of a hand dominated takeaway since the arms and hands are simply "along for the ride." There is no need to think about taking the clubhead back straight because the clubshaft and clubhead are pulled away from the ball due to waist and torso rotation that automatically keeps the arms and clubshaft "on plane." As the backswing continues, there is no need to worry about forcing the weight to stay in the inside of the right foot because the correct hip windup will not permit the player's weight slide laterally past the inside of the right foot.

As the backswing progresses, the player who is not hip dominated is concerned about making a full shoulder turn and keeping the swing arc wide to build power. These are movements that themselves are fraught with risks for swing imbalances and complications of thought. The hip dominated player realizes that a full wind up of the torso generated by a sound wind up of the right hip going back will automatically cause the shoulders to turn more fully and swing width will automatically be achieved due to a full wind up of the shoulders which is turn are largely due to a full wind up of the hips.

The player who lacks hip domination at the top of his or her swing will forever be searching for that "magic move" to transition into an effective downswing. High handicappers wonder if the secret to not coming over the top is a driving of right elbow into the side violently to swing "inside out" or to forcefully shift the weight over to the left foot regardless of whether the upper body may be pulled forward too. The better player will constantly be worried about getting "too quick" at the top of the swing and be constantly fighting to capture that elusive tempo to once and for all conquer the dreaded hook without giving in to pushing the ball right.

By contrast, the player who is hip dominated at the top of the swing knows that the clubshaft plane going back to the ball will be more or less correct because an aggressive unwinding of the left hip automatically pulls the hands back into the "slot" to deliver the clubhead into the ball from inside the target line path, and knows that the clubface will square up without a roll over of the hands and wrists.

How a hip dominated swing can be developed will be discussed in the following chapters. But before we begin our search for a stronger and more reliable golf swing, it is appropriate to ask a litmus test question. How can we be sure a hip dominated swing is consistent with sound swing fundamentals developed by leading teachers of the golf swing and leading players over the years? Is a hip dominated swing a new fad or a harebrained theory, which, if pursued, could actually undermine the current skill level of your golf swing? Or can it form the basis of a unified method of swinging a golf club that embraces the key ideas and knowledge of not only outstanding teachers, but great golfers who have put their swings to the test of both time and top level competition? To gain a more fuller understanding of the place hip domination has in golf swing theory, let's take a look at some basic physics, and then look at what some of the greats have to say about the movement of the golfer's hips and their essential role and function in the golf swing.

THE CASE FOR HIP TO HIP ™ METHODOLOGY

The Human Skeleton and Geometry

While reviewing numerous golfing magazine tips and instructional articles and books, I discovered a recurring pattern of writing that seemed odd. Most of the literature would focus on various movements to make during the golf swing.

The articles would include such topics as how a player should take the clubhead back, how the player should make a full shoulder turn, how the player should turn the hips, how far a player should swing the club back, how the player should swing his or her arms going back during the backswing and coming back during the downswing, how the swing plane should be more upright or flatter, how the player should keep his or her balance, how to avoid swaying, and how to keep your head still. But most of the writing focused only upon each particular part of the golf swing as if it were unto itself, and a separate topic of consideration and focus. Almost every book and article omitted focus on any type of overall, unified method to follow in making the golf swing function as a whole, or as a single athletic move over a 1.5 second time period.

For example, many magazine tips and even comprehensive instructional books covering the entire swing discussed the shoulder turn as though it were an isolated and separate subject. The admonition that power can be generated with the adoption of a "full shoulder turn" is fundamentally basic and a point that enjoys universal agreement. But how to make a full shoulder turn IN RELATION TO THE REST OF THE MOVING PARTS of the golf swing was often not addressed. Similarly, swing plane discussion tend to focus on the steepness of the arm swing as though it was a topic unto itself, but hardly ever was there any mention of the arm swing plane in relation to the other moving parts of the swing.

One of the more paradoxical issues in all of golf swing literature is the turn of the hips and its relationship to the turn of the shoulders. Many of the instructional materials would admonish the student to make a full shoulder turn, but restrict the turn of the hips. Some instructors have referred to this technique as "building coil." The theory is that greater tension can be built by restricting the turn of the hips while turning the shoulders as fully as possible, thereby generating more power into the downswing. Indeed, none other than Ben

Hogan advocated this concept in his writings. Having spent a large part of my youth trying to pull this technique off, I have always wondered why it always seemed so hard to do this, and why the strain that seemed to dominate my mind at the top of my golf swing also seemed to be more of a distracting type of thought occurring in the middle of my downswing, which at best seemed ill timed.

As I studied the swings of more and more top pros and experimented with my own swing, however, I realized that the goal of coil, at least in the sense of having the hips actually working against the shoulders during the course of the backswing, was not only mentally distracting, but also physically impossible. And if we take a few moments to think about it, the reason is very simple.

All we have to do is think a little about the human anatomy, and the human skeleton and we can make some progress in getting to an answer. The idea of "coil" in the sense of building tension between the shoulders and the hips by fully turning the shoulder during the backswing while simultaneously restricting the turn of the hips suggests a level of pent up or built up MUSCLE TENSION. But the human skeleton is built in manner by which the pelvis and hips are rigidly connecting to a person's spine, bone to bone, which, bone to bone, is equally connected, rigidly, to that person's shoulder blades.

We are not talking about soft tissue. The interrelationship between a person's shoulder blades, backbone and pelvis involves not high tolerance, high variance "play" between the circular movements of these parts, but instead is a rigid, hard mechanical set of connections. From a skeletal point of view, the degree of shoulder turn is extremely calibrated to the degree of pelvis rotation. It is true that some shoulder rotation can occur without any corresponding rotation of the pelvis, but it is very low, perhaps 30-40 degrees at most. If that is so in the skeletal world, how can a player make a 90-degree shoulder turn by restricting his or her hip turn? To achieve a 90-degree shoulder turn, the player MUST turn his or hips during the backswing at least 50-60 degrees!

Many instructional books advocate that the "ideal" type of turn is a 90-degree shoulder turn accompanied by a 45-degree hip turn. But pure skeletal geometric readings demonstrate that this is impossible! This leads me to conclude that, on the basis of plain skeletal anatomy, the ONLY WAY TO MAKE A FULL SHOULDER TURN DURING THE BACKSWING IS BY MAKING A HIP TURN OF AT LEAST 50-60 DEGREES.

If such a full hip turn is anatomically required to make the full 90 degree turn of the shoulders during the backswing, the question remains why do so many instructional books recommend a restriction of the hips? My view is that the overemphasis of "coil" was spawned by one of the greatest players of all time, arguably the most brilliant shotmaker ever and one of the most gifted geniuses of all time on the subject of golf swing theory—Ben Hogan. And until very recently, the notion of a restricted hip turn was thought by many to be a worthwhile goal in the pursuit of a better golf swing.

Hogan published one of the all time great instructional books in 1957, *Five Lessons: The Modern Fundamentals of Golf,* which was the culmination of a series of five magazine articles Hogan wrote for Sports Illustrated earlier that year. In Five Lesson, Hogan articulated what many believe to be some of the most important statements about how the golf swing works. By far, most of the text Hogan wrote still holds true today as a seminal articulation of bedrock golf swing fundamentals. Some of his ideas were pioneering, such as the notion of the swing plane analogized to a pane of glass from the golfer's neck to the ball to define the angle of the swing circle. Many of Hogan's ideas are still the basic starting point in any sound analysis and discussion of swing fundamentals.

Hogan also had numerous important observations to make about the role of the hips in the swing, which many golf teachers and students today still believe as gospel truth. We will consider some of Hogan's critical observations about hip turn in more detail shortly. However, one of the key points Hogan made about his hips in *Five Lessons* missed the mark.

Hogan believed that during his backswing, he restricted his hip turn while turning his shoulders as fully as possible, thereby creating what he called coil, which was a stretching of the muscles between the hips and the shoulders. This stretch or coil in Hogan's view created a rubber band effect whereby the energy stored up by "coiling" in this fashion during the backswing could be simply released during the downswing by a turn of the left hip back to the target, which would cause the shoulders, arms and hands to unwind quickly, thereby generating powerful clubhead speed.

Hogan's assertions about his professed restricted hip turn during the backswing are certainly unequivocal, but they raise several interesting questions. First, assuming for sake of argument that Hogan did have a restricted hip turn, or at least tried to have one, is an attempt to restrict the hip turn during the backswing smart for most other golfers? Second, did Hogan in fact really restrict his hips in the way he claimed? If Hogan did not restrict his hips as he claimed, what are the instructional implications of a fuller hip turn? Even if for the sake of argument we can assume that Hogan did restrict his hips (a very dubious assumption), a serious question is whether anyone who does not play golf 8 hours per day has the athletic flexibility to pull this unnatural feat off. And if it is not smart or practical to follow Hogan's advice from an athletic point of view, and a fuller backswing hip turn is wise, is there any reliable method that can be used in developing a fuller hip turn?

Golf instructor David Ledbetter examined some of these issues in his insightful book published in 2000, The *Fundamentals of Hogan*. Using newly discovered photographs of Hogan taken by Anthony Ravielli and obtained by his publisher, Ledbetter undertook a comprehensive, detailed analysis of all of Hogan's writings, including *Five Lessons,* for the purpose of writing a modern perspective about the current body of golf swing knowledge and theory as it has evolved from Hogan's instructional classics. The result is a complete up to date re-examination of Hogan's teachings and an inquiry into which of Hogan's theories have stood the test of time, which of Hogan's ideas mesh with modern golf swing theory and instruction, and which of his ideas have come and gone out of favor.

On the subject of the role of hips during the backswing, Ledbetter discusses Hogan's beliefs about his restricted hip turn and coil, and notes that Hogan had an extremely high degree of muscular flexibility conducive to an exceptional amount of "wind up" during the backswing and torque while keeping his head still, athletic feats which he observed most golfers would find difficult to achieve. Ledbetter advocates that his preferred way to get "wound up" during the backswing is to keep the right knee flexed and solid, and states that "By doing this you will not have to consciously retard or "restrain" the hip movement to get wound up, as Hogan put it"

Ledbetter did not stop there, however. He went on to say "I think it's all but impossible, and very uncomfortable, to curtail the turn of the hips while at the same time trying to turn the shoulders fully; there's a relationship between them, after all, and only a very flexible person could try to do this. Hogan was certainly flexible, *but it is apparent in photographs of him that [Hogan] turned his hips far more that he thought he did."*

Ledbetter's observations about Hogan's backswing hip turn are very significant. They prove that what Hogan believed about his degree of hip turn during the backswing and what actually happened during his backswing were two different things! Furthermore, Ledbetter clearly advocates against someone actually trying to restrict his or her hip turn during the backswing. But he nonetheless expressed a view that "coil" or getting "would up" with the use of a stable right knee could still be achieved.

The compelling need for a full and complete turn or windup of the hips to the top of the backswing has been stressed by a top teacher as recently as January, 2004. In a very recent issue of *Golf Digest*, Jim McLean, arguably one of the most insightful teachers in America, discusses how a restricted hip turn undermines a good, full backswing. In a tip feature, he discussed two illustrations, one with a restricted hip turn, and one with a full hip turn, and commented how the restricted turn impeded the generation of power on the downswing. He makes the frank admission that some of his earlier teachings about the so called "X Factor," whereby he advocated as much separation as possible from the left shoulder to the hips to generate power, may have caused some players to improperly restrict their hip turns. He stressed that the shoulders and hips are connected and that a full hip turn formed the basis of a full shoulder turn.

The differences in the two swing illustrations in the *Golf Digest* lesson by Jim McLean are striking. Jim's point was that a coil of the shoulders over the hips could produce good tension and torque leading into the downswing even with a full hip turn. One of the most striking images of the two illustrations was how much the player's belt buckle had turned. In the restricted hip turn swing, the player's belt buckle was not much turned away from the ball. But in the full hip turn illustration, the player's BELT BUCKLE, OR BELLY BUTTON HAD FULLY ROTATED BACK FROM THE BALL TO THE POINT OF BEING DIRECTLY OVER THE PLAYER'S RIGHT FOOT. Does your belt buckle rotate, or belly button, fully rotate until it is directly over your right foot at the top of your backswing? Take heed of Jim McLean's point about fully turning your hips and see whether your swing improves.

THE CRITICAL IMPORTANCE OF HIP TURN
IN SWING INSTRUCTION: A HISTORICAL REVIEW

If there is any truth to my view that golf instruction is too complicated and focused on hyper-mechanical movements of the hands, wrists, arms, clubshaft and clubhead, the alternative swing theory focus, on shoulders and hips, and primarily on the hips, must be based on well grounded thinking by those who know best—legendary golfers. Without a historical basis of theoretical support, the ideas expressed in this book amount to little more than more than another set of fad ideas to heap onto the mountain of fad ideas we now have.

I earnestly believe the historical level of support for a new method of emphasis exists, and that we only need to listen to, or at least objectively analyze, what the best swingers of all time have to say on the subject. Let's take a closer look at what the all time great players have had to say about the importance of hip turn to the golf swing.

Bobby Jones and the Role of Hips

To Bobby Jones, the very essence of the golf swing was using the hips as the swing's basic foundation and the engine driving every part of the swing's motion.

Let's focus on the takeaway first. Should you take the clubhead back with your hands, arms or clubhead to start the swing? Many teaching professionals advocate these types of techniques to initiate the swing. But Bobby Jones, who arguably had the most graceful, beautiful and tempo-laden golf swing in history, strongly believed otherwise as a fundamental matter. In a collection of his writings about how to play golf entitled *Bobby Jones on Golf*, he left no doubt about his view of how to start the golf swing. Jones said, "That the first motion of the backswing should be made by the legs or hips there can be little doubt. To start it with the hands results inevitably in the lifting upright motion characteristic of the beginner who swings the club as though it were an axe, elevating it to the shoulder position without a semblance of the weight shift and shoulder turn effected by the professional" (*Bobby Jones on Golf*, Revised Edition 1997 by Sidney L. Matthew).

In 1998, golf book publisher American Golfer, Inc. asked Ben Crenshaw to review previously undiscovered instructional swing photos and yellow pad notes created by and belonging to Bobby Jones, which were found among Jones's papers at his Atlanta law firm. Crenshaw wrote a remarkable golf swing instructional book with Jones as a posthumous co-author, using side by side and frame by frame swing sequence photos comparing Crenshaw's own swing with Jones's swing, and placing Jones's frame by frame swing commentary alongside Crenshaw's own analysis of the swing sequence photos and using Jones's old notes. In the book, *Classic Instruction,* Crenshaw included comparative takeaway shots, and stated that Jones followed the usual technique then followed with hickory shafted clubs by drawing the hands back first and having the clubhead lag behind, in contrast to the modern technique of a one piece takeaway. In his analysis, Crenshaw stated that Jones's hands "move first". But Crenshaw surely did not mean that Jones's hands started the swing, but must have meant that the hands go back in Jones's swing before the clubhead.

Jones himself addressed what moved first in the takeaway. It is critical. Jones was quoted as saying, "The backswing movement originated in the center of the body. One has the feeling that the club is being pushed back by the left side and hand." The most distinguishing feature of Jones's takeaway with the fairway woods compared to Crenshaw's, however drew no comment. Crenshaw's takeaway is clearly one piece, but Jones's hips have rotated far more than Crenshaw's, even to the point that Jones's left heel is already being raised off the ground! In the photo sequence showing Jones and Crenshaw during the takeaway of long irons, Jones remarks, "The drag away from the ball. The clubhead lags because *the hips and* legs start the movement while the hands and wrists are relaxed." There is no doubt that Jones started his takeaway with his waist or midsection, by winding the hips first. It is the winding of Jones's hips from the very beginning that literally dragged his passive hands, clubshaft and clubhead along for the ride.

In the next photo sequence about half way into the backswing, Jones notes that "The swing progresses for some distance before the hands begin to elevate the club and the first cocking of the wrists becomes apparent." Thus, in Jones's swing, his hands and therefore his arms also do not even get into the act of moving or driving the backswing almost half way into the backswing. Further evidence of this delayed involvement of the arms and hands is shown on pages 54 and 55 of *Classic Instruction,* which compares down the line from behind photos comparing Ben Crenshaw's swing with a long iron to Bobby Jones's long iron swing. There Jones is shown to have made a very deep turn of the hips going back to the point that his left heel is off the ground and a gap can be seen between Jones's knees, in contrast to Crenshaw's hip turn.

But it is Jones's observations of his backswing halfway back that is most revealing. He says, "The right elbow meanwhile keeps close to the side, but it is not cramped against the ribs. "THE RIGHT ARM IS COMPLETELY RELAXED WHILE THE LEFT PUSHES THE CLUB BACK IN A WIDE ARC." Finally, the photo shows Jones hips almost fully coiled, and his shoulders almost fully turned at this point. Here, the right arm is completely relaxed and has not even become involved in Jones's backswing, even though Jones's hips and shoulders have almost finished their work! Indeed, by the lights of Jones's clubhead, his swing is half way finished, but in terms of hip and shoulder turn, Jones has almost completed his backswing at this point!

Looking at the two sets of photos together and combining his statements, we can observe that Bobby Jones initiated his backswing solely with a rotational winding of the hips while keeping his hands and arms totally passive, and his right arm completely relaxed with no involvement whatsoever in the swing until half way into his backswing after his hips and shoulders had almost completely finished winding up!

My thesis is that the hickory shaft aspect of Bobby Jones's swing has been greatly overstated as an exclusive explanation of the clubhead lag, and it overshadows the relationship between the start of Jones's swing and completion of most of his backswing. The very foundation of Jones's swing rests not on his hands going back before the clubhead, which results in a clubhead lag, but on his hips and shoulders turning almost completely, with a little late help from his left hand and arm, before his right arm ever becomes involved with his swing.

In my view, it is not the hickory shaft feature that means anything. It is both the fact that Jones's hips were the driving force of his backswing, and the fact that, *as a timing, tempo, swing plane and swing movement sequence issue, Jones finished winding his hips and shoulders before using his right arm to complete his backswing. In other words, Jones never used either arm or hand during the takeaway, and never used his right arm or shoulder muscles in his backswing until his hips and shoulders finished their backswing windup.* As the rest of the book will show, using this sequence of movement as a governor to drive the backswing will successfully create swing plane, coil and indeed, even swing tempo and timing.

Jack Nicklaus and Hips

Jack Nicklaus, who holds the greatest career record in golf history, has always valued a strong, effective winding and unwinding action of the hips. In his book, *My Golden Lessons*, Jack related that he learned from his teacher, Jack Grout, that hip action was rotational, much like a cylinder turning back and forth. To accomplish a good full hip turn, Jack focused on winding his right hip back to create the effect of torque producing coil.

Later in this book, we will examine the use of a draw of the right hip to help with hip turn during the backswing.

Jack also has an astute appreciation for the nuance in the sequence of hip action in starting the swing. In *My Golden Lessons,* Jack compares starting the golf swing with the method of using a lag of the clubhead following a drag of the hands away, with the method of employing a wrist cock takeaway and with the method known as the one piece takeaway. Jack expresses a personal preference between the lag technique and the one piece takeaway. The significance of his observations on this issue is reflected in his keen observation about the "lag" method as the one demonstrated by old photos of Bobby Jones's swing. Since Jones clearly started his backswing with his hip turn away from the ball, Jack's partial use of the lag method is important in that respect.

Tiger Woods and Hips

As time continues and as more great players in the game of golf emerge, we will gain better and better insight into the swing techniques that really work. Tiger Woods and his swing philosophies are no exception. Following his historic and dramatic major championship victories in 2000 and 2001 beginning with his U.S. Open win at Pebble Beach and culminating with the "Tiger Slam" of winning all four majors in a row with his 2001 Masters victory, Tiger explained his swing methods in *How I Play Golf,* published in 2001. Tiger's "how to" manual goes through the entire bag, beginning with his how to's for putting and the short game, on to drives, fairway woods, and irons, and mental preparation, focus and strategy.

In describing his six keys to a great backswing, Tiger, like Hogan, mentions his desire to restrict his hip turn by keeping his left heel on the ground to create more torque. Interestingly, the photo showing Tiger at the top of his swing shows that his right hip has turned considerably. But Tiger makes another point that I consider to be extremely important.

One of Tiger's six keys to a great backswing is that, in his words, "My weight is gathered onto my right heel." In my view, Tiger's expression of this idea is somewhat of a breakthrough in golf swing fundamentals. This is at first blush a "balance" point that was not directly addressed in Hogan's *Five Lessons.* Bobby Jones did not address it in his writings, nor did Ben Crenshaw address it in his book with Jones, or by Ledbetter in his *Fundamentals of Hogan.* Why can this be so significant? In my view, the loading of weight onto the right heel at the top of the backswing is not only a balancing rule, it is the most reliable technique to avoid swaying the upper body weight during the backswing outside the right foot. I believe it is a new way, or at least newly articulated way, to simultaneously maintain excellent balance throughout the entire swing, while guaranteeing a correct wind up movement of the right hip during the backswing.

More importantly, if this concept is blended with Bobby Jones's method of starting the takeaway with a rotation of the center of the body and a winding of the hips, the flow of weight onto the right heel can provide an integrated foundation of the backswing that guarantees a full turn of the hips and shoulders, achieves proper balance and imposes a certain element of tempo excellence that seems to happen by itself. Unification during the backswing of the hip turn, takeaway, balance and tempo, both physically and mentally, can greatly improve your swing and your swing learning curve! In fact, Tiger Woods on page 124 of *How I Play Golf* expressly states that "I UNIFY MY BACKSWING."

Another revealing aspect of Tiger Wood's golf swing is the degree to which he actually clears his hips toward to the target at impact. On page 138 of *How I Play Golf,* the first middle photo sequence shows that at impact, Tiger's left leg has almost totally straightened and his belt buckle is totally facing the target. His hips have unwound to the point that the front of both of his thighs are facing down a line parallel to the target line. In the rear view sequence below, you can see both buttons on the back of Tiger's rear pants pockets. This is clear and convincing evidence that his downswing hip rotation back to the target is fully complete at the moment of impact.

It is absolutely clear that Tiger Woods is aggressively using his hip turn through the impact zone to square up his clubface down the target line. Another way to say Hogan's secret was the fastest possible clearing of the hips during the downswing is that both Ben Hogan and Tiger Woods squared up their clubface at impact not by using any snap or roll of their hands and wrists but by aggressively posting up their left legs and fully clearing their hips.

Hogan, Hips and The "Secret"

Despite the contradiction concerning the actual windup of Ben Hogan's hips during the backswing, and the purported restriction of hip turn that Hogan incorrectly believed he employed during his backswing, Hogan's statements about the role of the hips during the downswing hit the mark. In fact, Ben Hogan's description of the movement of his hips during the downswing and his statements concerning the importance of the hips getting back to the ball are widely if not universally accepted as the most profound pronouncements about golf swing fundamentals ever made. In *Five Lessons*, Hogan placed a tremendous amount of emphasis on his downswing hip movement.

Hogan believed that from a "wound up" or "coiled" position at the top of the backswing, the downswing was initiated and driven with his hips. He meticulously described the sequence of hip rotational mechanics that he observed happening during his downswing, as well as the feelings or sensations he personally felt as the downswing occurred. Hogan stated that his downswing started with a slight lateral shift of the hips that transferred his balance of weight onto his left foot; follow by a rapid rotation of the hips back to the target. In Hogan's view, this shifting and turning of the hips back to the target must drive the rest of the swing, with the shoulders, arms and hands following along behind the lead of the unwinding hips.

In *The Hogan Way*, published in 2000, author John Andrisani described a World of Golf videotape featuring Hogan in a match, in which the commentator was Grand Slam great Gene Sarazen. At the end of the match, Sarazen asked Hogan, "What's the most important thing in the swing?" Hogan replied, "You must let the lower body lead the downswing—the hips and the knees—then release the club near the bottom. Most amateurs rotate the shoulders first, causing them to hit across the ball and hit the outside of it instead the back of it." To Hogan, the forceful leading of the downswing with a strong and aggressive rotation of the hips over the left foot was the most important move in the golf swing. The was the essence of Hogan's "secret."

In *Five Lessons*, Hogan also stated that the hips should clear out, through the swift rotation of the left hip around and out of the way of the impact zone, as "quickly as possible." David Ledbetter in The Fundamentals of Hogan echoes this view. Concerning the hips unwinding toward the target, Ledbetter aptly observed, "In Hogan's opinion, the faster the hips turn, the better." Of course, Hogan's precise descriptions of how the hips lead the downswing and unwind rapidly do not fully describe some of the techniques the student can employ to actually improve his or her downswing hip turn, nor does he provide a detailed description of the feeling sensations he felt as all of this occurred. Later chapters of this book, however, will focus more on these points to hopefully help you get your hips moving like Hogan's or like the hip rotations of many of today's top amateurs and professionals.

Many swing teachers have cautioned beginners against focusing too heavily on this statement at the risk of worsening coming over the top. In my view, and as the remainder of this book will explain, this fear has been over exaggerated and has overlooked the real causes of coming over the top, arm and shoulder domination from the top and failing to get weight at the beginning of the downswing quickly back to the left foot. In this author's view, when Hogan said the shifting and turning as quickly as possible of the hips leading the downswing was the most critical part of the golf swing, he meant it, and it is as true today as it was when Hogan said it.

The Hips and Sam Snead

Probably no better example of how well the hips can shown to work in a magnificent golf swing is the swing of Sam Snead. His career record of wins and major championship victories was indeed incredible and spanned so many decades. But Slammin Sammy is also known for having one of the most smooth and beautiful golf swings in history. His swing was not only very powerful, but had a tempo about it that was sheer poetry. In his prime his big windup and turn flowed in a syrupy fashion into his downswing and a finish and follow through that was simply elegant.

But the most interesting aspect of Sam Snead's swing can be observed by carefully studying his swing photographed with a sequence camera. He obviously demonstrates a big pivot of his hips on his backswing and the lift of his left heel off the ground going back shows how big of a hip turn he produced. But the most fascinating thing about Sam Snead's hip turn was its SEQUENCE. A careful, close examination of Sam Snead's backswing clearly shows that his big hip turn and windup during his backswing was FULLY COMPLETED by the time his hands and arms reached hip high level only half way back into his backswing.

In other words, although Sam Snead's hands and arms have only swung halfway back into the radius of their backswing, Snead's hips had already finished their big windup fully. Once Snead's arms are only half way back into his backswing, his hips have fully wound themselves up! This is extremely revealing from the standpoint of not only the sequence of swing mechanics during the backswing, but the creation and establishment of swing tempo on the grand level of someone like Sam Snead. These topics will be explored more fully as the Hip to Hip Method is articulated later in this book. THE POINT, HOWEVER, IS THAT SAM SNEAD'S SWING IS PROOF POSITIVE THAT THE HIPS WIND UP FULLY WAY BEFORE THE ARMS AND HANDS FINISH MOVING TO THE TOP DURING THE BACKSWING!

I strongly submit that a careful analysis of Sam Snead's golf swing not only fully corroborates Bobby Jones's theories about the start and sequence of the backswing with the lead of the hips, it firmly establishes the principle that COMPLETELY WINDING UP THE HIPS FIRST DURING THE BACKSWING IS THE SINE QUA NON OF A TRULY WONDERFUL GOLF SWING. Many golfers over the years have marveled at Snead's "sit down" look half way into his downswing as a blueprint for a strong powerful unwinding of the hips during the downswing. Many touring pros actually try to emulate Snead's sit down look and spend a lot of time trying to figure out how to get that move down. Perhaps Snead's full windup of his hips as a first priority of his backswing may explain how he achieved the sit down look more than any other factor in his swing.

Other Notable Comments About The Hips

There is much more corroboration concerning the critical importance and crucial role of the hips during the golf swing. Numerous leading instructors and star players over the years have commented about the hips. Cataloging all of the comments and ideas, good and bad, would be redundant. However, suffice it to say that while the importance of the hips turning and unwinding rests on almost universal agreement, the day to day instructional focus upon them falls short.

FOCUSING ON HIPS SIMPLIFIES SWING LEARNING

One of the most important reasons why focusing on the hips for guidance in learning and improving your golf swing, is that it promotes a level of simplicity in swing analysis that is very effective. Swinging a golf club, as the description of a complex mechanical activity, is one of the most complicated and sophisticated athletic endeavors in all of sport. But the complexity of the golf swing does not necessarily mean that we clutter our minds with endless analysis, fads, swing cures, or instruction from every corner of the globe.

Simplicity does not have to mean a lack of sophistication or understanding about how a good golf swing fundamentally works. Indeed, I submit, that a unified focus on the hips using an approach like Hip to Hip can provide a level of integration into the athletic attempt to do something very complicated. The Hip to Hip Method of thinking about the golf swing transcends all of the picky and distracting details of all of the supposed moving parts. Some further explanation is warranted to better explain how simplifying the analysis of a golf swing can make it more effective.

The Three Basic Elements of Muscle Movement in a Golf Swing

If we put the whole body of golf swing theory and instruction aside for a moment and just look at what part of our bodies are "moving" during a golf swing, there are really only three sets of muscles at work:

1. THE HIPS;

2. THE SHOULDERS; and

3. THE ARMS, WRISTS and HANDS.

I combine the arms, wrists and hands into one set of muscles for several reasons. First, it is easier conceptually to simplify the golf swing and categorize the problems and solutions into one of three points of focus. Second, because the actual movement of the arms hands and wrists tend to interact closely with the clubshaft and clubhead as a set of hinging mechanisms, using the clubhead and clubshaft as focal points of instruction in reality implicates those muscles alone.

In contrast, the shoulder turn is one simple rotational body motion. The winding and unwinding of the hips is also one simple set of rotational motions. Focusing on the simple mechanical turning of the hips (which in turn rotate the shoulders for the first part of the swing), and the shoulders, (which pulls the right arm and the clubshaft back simply by being connected to the right shoulder) is much, much easier to learn than sophisticated and overly complex hand and clubhead movements.

There is much debate about whether the moves associated with the arms, hands and wrists should happen consciously, and if consciously, how to make them happen. I suggest that these hinging parts—the arms, hands and wrists, attract way too much attention. The arms, hands and wrists can move consciously, but as this book will show, need not, and for sake of simplicity most likely should not. There is plenty of widely accepted teaching application, that the proper cocking and uncocking of the player's wrists can naturally occur as a result of the centrifugal pull of the clubshaft and clubhead as the larger body muscles of the hips and shoulders swing the arms back and forth. So if focusing on the hips can in theory strengthen the rest of the moving parts of your golf swing, what are some of the actual advantages of doing so?

Focus on the Movement of the Hips, And the Shoulders and the Rest Will Follow

Given the proper rotational winding and unwinding of the hips, and their closely connected and interdependent partners, the shoulders, then the arms, hands, clubshaft and clubhead will follow along just nicely. This will enable you to unclutter your mind about a host of mechanical problems or issues that need not exist. For example, if the backswing is started by the clockwise winding up of the hips using some of the turning and drawing techniques discussed later in this book, there is really no need to worry about whether the clubhead is being taken back "straight" from the ball, or "outside" or "inside." The reason is that a correct backturn of the hips will automatically pull on the shoulders, causing them to turn on the correct pathway during the backswing, which in turn will cause the elbows and hands to travel along the correct backswing pathway. You can forget worrying about taking the clubhead back straight so long as your alignment is correct!

Likewise, if your attention during the takeaway and three quarters the way into the backswing is focused on fully winding up the hips and then completing whatever little shoulder turn there is left to complete, the arms, heretofore in a relaxed state, will automatically travel along the correct swing plane, leaving only a slight, passive cocking of the wrists at the top of the backswing, created mostly by the mere centrifugal force of the clubshaft to finish off the backswing. This eliminates the need to make artificial moves to steepen or flatten your swing plane because the full body rotational motion previously generated by your hips and shoulders will have done most all of the work!

The Hips Start to Govern Clubface Impact Position

Likewise, by focusing on insuring that the left hip truly leads the downswing by aggressively unwinding, to create a flash of speed in the clearing of the hips through the impact zone, you will (assuming correct alignment and grip settings) almost guarantee that the clubface, delivered into the back of the ball from a correct, inside pathway, will square up at impact. You can begin to eliminate the heave ho, or over the top motion, in the case of a beginner or high handicapper, or the dreaded wrist roll that haunts all low handicappers who dread the next bad hook.

Why the Hips Stabilize the Golf Swing

Probably the most important effect of mastering solid hip turn back and forth is the effect it will have upon your balance and your spinal stability. Your hips and trunk, which includes the bottom of your spine and your waist, is the center of gravity as the swing takes place. Going back during the backswing, the flywheel comprising the shoulders, arms and clubshaft revolves around your spine in a wide rotational fashion that is neither fully horizontal nor fully vertical. It is almost universally agreed that except for the rotational movement of the spine and thus the shoulders, the spine must remain stable and not move from side to side or up and down during the swing. Instead, the flywheel mechanism of the shoulders, arms, hands, and clubshaft must rotate reliably around the spine in a powerful manner. The arms themselves are not sources of power because the golf swing is not an athletic action like chopping wood or swinging a sledgehammer. If the arms were really sources of power, it would be possible to hit a golf ball 250-300 yards from a sitting position. The real source of power in a golf swing is the kinetic, rotational energy built up out of the ground, which flows outward eventually into the clubhead that it moving at the outer edge of the "arc" of the flywheel.

To generate the proper amount of rotational velocity by centrifugal force out from the spine to the arms and in turn to the clubshaft and clubhead, there must be a solid resistance against which the kinetic energy of spinal rotation and shoulder rotation can move. The only solid resistance against which to turn this big circular flywheel is the ground. How can the ground, which is totally flat and "horizontal," properly dissipate its centrifugal power out from the spine and shoulders into the outer reaches of the arc and ultimately to the clubhead, all of which resembles a semi horizontal, semi vertical flywheel? It is accomplished only by providing the rotational energy that flows up from the ground, into the legs, which transmit the ground's kinetic energy into the shoulder and arms through the rotation of the hips.

The only way to rotate the spine while keeping it stable is by focusing on a solid hip movement which is itself stable, so that the correct rotational movement of the spine can be accomplished in a manner which insures that the spine rotates, but remains stable and does not cause the arc of the flywheel to wobble or fly off track. If the hips wind and unwind correctly, your balance will fall into line, and your spine angle will be correctly maintained.

In fact, an excellent hip rotation back and through will actually create the type of spinal stability and strong, dynamic balance that is absolutely essential to hit powerful, and consistent golf shots, not vice versa. Strong swing balance and spinal stability are essential to insure that the rotational power of the flywheel be maximized while at the same time harnessed in a manner that keeps the arc of the clubhead on track. The only body movement connecting all of this to the ground, which is the source of rotational power in a golf swing, is the turn of the hips.

The Hips Create Shoulder Turn

On the other side of the golf swing's center of gravity, the hips, are the arms and shoulders. The shoulders can turn very little on their own. To see this for yourself, try sitting down on a stool, with your back straight and your arms crossed in front of you, and without moving your hips, turn your shoulders clockwise as far as you can turn them. Keep your eye on your left shoulder. You will see with your own eyes that the absolute most you can turn your shoulders all alone is about 20-30 degrees, and maybe 35 degrees but only if the arms pull the shoulders around somewhat. If this is so, how can most golf instructors recommend that a top-level backswing have about 90 degrees of shoulder turn at the top of the backswing? It is because the other 60 to 70 degrees of shoulder turn depends for the most part upon further rotational turn of the hips.

The Hips, Not the Arms, Generate Power

Power in a golf swing flows from centrifugal force, built up by the leverage created from unwinding your hips and shoulders on the downswing and the torque that rotation brings to bear on passively increasing wrist cock on the way down. Power does not flow from the muscles in either the upper or lower arms. Assuming you do not pick the clubhead up going back and keep your left arm straight going back to maintain a naturally wide arc (things you should not have to think about with a full turn of the shoulder and hips), power should be viewed as an automatic by product of a good full swing.

IS THE HIP TO HIP METHOD A PANACEA?

The Hip to Hip Method is not a cure all panacea for all golfers, because there may be serious swing problems (such as bobbing or lunging) in need of correction unrelated to the motion of a player's hips. But Hip to Hip can be a successful system for golfers of any skill level. Better players who rely on timing to square up the clubface at impact are often surprised to find that the problem is not really timing, but mechanics. Good players can learn to improve consistency dramatically by learning to rely on using the hips and torso rotating through the ball at impact in a flash to square up the clubface to the target line.

CHAPTER 3

PRE-SWING FUNDAMENTALS: POSTURE, ALIGNMENT, SETUP AND GRIP

Before we begin our journey toward a stronger golf swing by using the Hip to Hip Method, a few pre-swing fundamentals are in order. A good golf swing will not result in a good golf shot unless it is matched with an equally sound and effective set up and address to the ball. The fundamentals of good posture, good alignment and ball positioning and good grip are essential. A lot has been written about how to go about these critical pre-swing fundamentals with the familiar mountain of fads and tips. Let's try to keep it very simple but work toward some pre-swing methodology that consistently works over and over and over.

Address Posture

Unless you stand properly at address, you simply cannot make a good swing. Okay fine, good posture is essential. But how?

This does not have to be complicated. To have good posture, you must be well balanced, with your weight smack between the balls and heels of your feet, your back must be relatively straight and your arms should hang naturally from your shoulders with only the help of gravity. This means soft, loose arms at address, not ramrod stiff ax handles. But again, how can we do it right time after time after time?

The formula that always works, for you, me and everyone is "CUBOAH." It really is this simple—chin up, butt out, arms hanging. How straight should your back be? However straight it is when you balance your weight between the heels and balls of your feet with your knees slightly flexed, and you actually stick your butt out. I mean stick it out or jut it out. How high should your chin be? However high it can be without your neck being stiff and your eyesight to the ball as relaxed as you can be. How far should you stand from the ball? Whatever distance results when you literally drop your arms while holding the club with your hands at your waist, standing perfectly straight up, and pointing the club straight up, and having stuck your chin up and your butt out, letting your arms drop as softly and as relaxed as they can drop the clubhead onto the ground. Illustration 3.1 shows how the use of chin up, butt out and arms hang, or CUBOAH, promotes excellent posture.

At address, your arms should "be as noodles" dangling from your shoulders and the clubhead should be behind the ball from whatever distance you stand in a TOTALLY relaxed fashion from the ball with your butt out and your chin up. Right before takeaway, your arms should be completely relaxed and limp. Jack Nicklaus in his instructional book, *My Golden Lesson,* advises players to let their shoulders totally relax to feel the arms go limp to make a full, fluid golf swing.

Are there any other more elaborate or sophisticated techniques to secure a better posture position, or to embrace any other type of swing theory or idea tailored to your particular build or height? Nope. Not at all. For all sizes of player with any type of build, the answer is CUBOAH, pure and simple. Confirmation can be found in Jack Nicklaus's instructional book entitled *My Golden Lessons.* There, Jack discusses how important it is to keep your spine angle stable during the swing, and recommends an address posture idea to insure it. He recommends, "As you set up to the ball, shove your butt back and out as far as it will go, then visualize yourself keeping it there throughout the swing."

Ill. 3.1—Chin Up, Arms Hang, Butt Out. This creates an excellent posture at address.

Alignment at Address

Assuming you want to hit a straight golf shot with a normally "straight swing path," you will want your hips, shoulders and feet (assuming both are pointed straight out at the ball, a point that is in need of some refinement in a moment) in a line, like the two rails of a railroad track, that is parallel to the target line or flight line of the golf ball to its intended target. The fundamental of parallel alignment for a straight golf shot is easy enough to comprehend, but the difficulty is in its application.

It is very difficult to see yourself at address and it is often wise to get a "checkup" occasionally from a trained friend or instructing pro to make sure your alignment is correct. Left to fester, bad alignment, even if it is only off a few tiny degrees, can actually lead to horrible swing habits, such as a loop in your backswing, coming over the top, or some other flawed attempt at mid-swing correction of a swing path flawed by the initial misalignment.

But apart from relying on someone else to look over your shoulder, how can you get in the habit of insuring that your alignment is perfect or near perfect day in and day out? Is it possible? The answer is a clear yes, if you are willing to adopt a very simple habit.

The habit is hitting practice range balls or warm up shots before a round, without exception, with the ball lying between two extra golf clubs that serve as the "railroad track" as your own visual aid. To make it really effective, take a third extra golf club, and lay it parallel to the two clubs serving as the ball's railroad tracks, but across the front of your feet. Illustration 3.2 makes the point. With the three clubs, you can easily measure, test and correct your alignment completely on every single shot. Every single shot serves to build an ingrained habit of you visually doing it right every single time, even on the course when you don't lay down those extra clubs.

Ill. 3.2—Railroad Tracks insure good alignment if you make this practice technique a habit.

Sometimes I only use the two clubs to frame in the golf ball as the railroad track if I feel comfortable that my feet are lining up very nicely. But if I feel on any given day the slightest deviation from what I can clearly see to be a perfect parallel set up, then I immediately pull out all three extra clubs.

Okay, you're thinking to yourself, that sounds like a hassle to remember to do this every time I hit balls. Won't I look goofy laying those clubs out on the range? The answer is no on both counts. If you really want to guarantee perfect parallel alignment, and are serious enough about wanting to improve your game, laying down the railroad tracks every single time will pay you more dividends than any other idea in this book. After you try it a few times on the range, and you see the overwhelmingly powerful results you will achieve from good, strong alignment, you will be hooked on this habit.

And who cares what someone else thinks about your technique on the range? Ben Hogan used to tuck a headcover under his right armpit to make sure he did not let his elbow fly during his backswing. Do you think Hogan cared what someone else thought about his practice habits? In truth, folks will start to talk behind your back about how careful and meticulous you are about your alignment, and, having heard it said about others who do it, I can assure you the talk takes on a tone of respect that in essence sends the message that you are one smart golfer.

Your Grip with Hip to Hip

There are volumes of excellent discussion about having a proper grip. Teachers more qualified than me have spoken well on the use of the overlapping grip versus the interlocking grip, and the need to grip the club in the palm of your left hand and the fingers of your right hand. I have only one point to make as to what I believe is a key fundamental. I recognize there are valid exceptions for extremely strong swings used by golfers such as Tiger Woods or Ben Hogan. But for the rest of the world, including top professionals, I think you should see at least three (3) knuckles on your left hand as your stand to the ball at address, gripping the club, and look down.

Why do I contend this is fundamental? Without a lot of very quick hand action, it is very difficult to square up the clubface with a weaker grip. The weaker grip tempts you to square up the clubface by rolling your wrists if your timing is off. Why not encourage the hips to open at impact, by forcing yourself to rely on your hips to square up the clubface rather than your hands? If your fear is that you will start hooking, that is a good thing. With a three (3) knuckle grip, if you do start hooking, your can rest assured you are trying to square the clubface up by rolling your wrists instead of turning your hips open. The three (3) knuckle grip actually almost forces you to start relying on your hips to bring the clubhead into the back of the ball at impact in order to avoid a hook, and that is the best problem you can ever possibly have.

Other Address Set Up Issues: Distribution of Weight, Setting Up "Behind the Ball" and Hand Location, and Ball Location

Another frequent question you may have about addressing the ball is how much weight should you have on your left foot and how much weight should you have on your right foot? I realize there are several schools of thought about weight distribution at address, and recognize that many modern teachers favor putting 60%-70% of your weight onto your right foot at address. The explanation is that this helps you load your turn onto your right side during the backswing, and setting it there before your backswing begins will better insure you have most of your weight onto your right foot as the backswing is completed to better "coil" up behind the ball. A related issue is whether you should set up "behind the ball" at address by dropping your right shoulder slightly and tilting your upper body slightly away from the target.

I do not advocate these types of set ups. One key reason I believe these set up techniques are problems is that they complicate your set up too much. How much do you set up behind the ball? Do you have 60%, 65% or 70% on your right foot? These are distractions that keep your focus on the real issues such as alignment, good sound posture, maintaining balance and a top-notch hip and shoulder turn. Why clutter your address up? Another reason I think these ideas are unnecessary is that if the hips and shoulders do their job properly during the backswing using the Hip to Hip Method, then you will be correctly coiled and loaded correctly onto your right side at the top of your backswing.

Under the Hip to Hip Method, I advocate that you keep your set up as simple as possible. Set up with you weight equally distributed between your left foot and right foot, and count on the wind up of your hips to get your weight loaded up onto your right heel at the top. And do not set up behind the ball. Stand over the ball straight up, leaning neither toward the target nor away from the target.

A related issue is the location of your hands at address. Should they be "ahead of" or "in front of the ball," "even with the ball," or "behind the ball?" In my view, your hands at address should be wherever they loosely hang, straight down. This means that your hands will be gripping the club together about right in front of your belly button, right in the middle of your body. In the case of short or medium irons, where the golf ball at address may be somewhat closer to the middle or middle front of your stance, the hands will be somewhat even with the ball. In the case of long irons, fairway woods and the driver, where you address the ball with its location between your feet being somewhere pretty close to your left heel or instep, your hands, being in front of your belly button, hanging nice and naturally, will tend to be somewhat "behind the ball."

Setting up at address with your hands directly in front of you will also help you maintain a better "one piece" takeaway driven by your hip and shoulder turn from the very beginning of your swing. Conversely letting your hands hang naturally right in front of your belly button will avoid a serious fault many beginning and intermediate golfers are guilty of, which is setting up with the hands in front of the ball, and starting the takeaway totally backwards by cocking the wrists to move the clubhead back, which in turn completely ruins your swing plane and turn of the large hip and shoulder muscles during the backswing.

"Priming the Pump" At Address: Waggling and Other Relaxation Ideas

Another pre-swing issue must be addressed. How do you get your backswing started? What is going to be your backswing "trigger?" And what is the routine you should follow before you trigger your backswing?

There are entire books and golf magazine articles that discuss the pre-swing routine, and the opinions are varied as to how you should warm yourself up once you address the ball in order to start your backswing. I will address the backswing "trigger" in the next chapter, but the issue here is how you "get the motor" going? Ben Hogan used a waggle of the clubhead at address to get his motor started, by holding the club slightly off the ground and, in a relaxed fashion, cocking the wrists back and forth, moving the clubhead back away from and back to the back of the golf ball. Hogan believed this was a very important aspect of starting his swing and he used it religiously.

Some golfers like to slightly lift the clubface off the ground while keeping the clubhead stationary without any waggle. Some players shrug their shoulders several times before takeaway.

I believe you should use whatever type of motor "warm up" habit that is natural and comfortable to you personally and that successfully enables you to make a smooth, unhurried backswing. The two critical keys are that you adopt a warm up technique that you rely upon swing after swing after swing, on the range and on the course, and that the technique helps you stay as comfortable as possible at address.

One type of swing motor "warm up" habit I would suggest you try if you have not totally adopted a reliable technique is based upon the entire thesis of this book that most golfers by far are most guilty of tensing up their grip and arms, both during address and during the backswing, rather than letting the shoulders, and primarily the hips, dominate the golf swing. As I will address in the following chapters, the arms can actually be very, very relaxed during the entire backswing and most of the downswing and still end up being the vehicles through which great power can be imparted into the back of a golf ball. To that end, I suggest that you consider focusing your full attention at address on loosening and relaxing your arms at address.

As you stand over the ball, even if you already use a good waggle to get yourself going, try keeping your arms as free and loose as possible. Focus on making your right shoulder as relaxed and soft as whip cream, with total relaxation and zero tension, while feeling your right elbow go completely limp, and feeling it dangle freely from your soft right shoulder. Feel your grip pressure relaxing, and especially feel your right hand grip softening to the point that you right hand feels like it is about to fall off your club. Feel your chest muscles relax fully and feel your wrists as they waggle the club in a loose, almost limp manner. These types of sensations can help tremendously in keeping your shoulders, arms and hands as soft and relaxed as possible at address, right before you take the club back and begin your backswing.

One of the key premises of the Hip to Hip method is that anything other than zero tension in your arms and shoulder muscles at address and even during your backswing is extremely harmful to your golf swing health! As the next chapter will show, keeping your shoulders, arms and hands so relaxed will lead you into a whole new way of swinging a golf club. Let's now turn to the Hip to Hip Method, and learn how it works.

CHAPTER 4

THE HIP TO HIP METHOD ™: TURNING THE HIPS, FROM START TO FINISH

Now that we have a good system pulled together to address the ball with good posture, stable and well centered balance, and full arm and shoulder relaxation, let's get the golf swing going. The golf world is chock full of diversity in the manner and type of golf swing players learn and adopt to play this game, and great success has been achieved by players having golf swings that were totally idiosyncratic, if not totally unorthodox. But in these pages that follow, we will consider a new type of golf swing method that I refer to as the Hip to Hip Method.

The type of golf swing that I describe when discussing the Hip to Hip method is actually not new, or in any sense different or revolutionary. It is what I sincerely believe to be merely a reflection of the so called "classic" golf swing that has been so successfully used down through the ages. The method is based on sound swing fundamentals of the type followed by greats such as Nicklaus, Hogan, Jones, Snead, and Tiger Woods. The Hip to Hip Method is really more of a method of instructional communication designed to help players of all ability levels seek improvement of their golf swings in terms of the classic fundamentals, and to help golfers make more effective progress in moving the right parts of the body at the right time so as to produce the type of swing that tends to work better and better, whatever the golfer's starting level of ability.

THE FUNDAMENTAL PREMISE OF THE HIP TO HIP METHOD IS THAT THERE IS NOT ENOUGH INSTRUCTIONAL EMPHASIS PLACED ON THE USE OF THE LARGE MUSCLES—THE HIPS AND SHOULDERS—IN THE GOLF SWING IN A UNIFIED SENSE, AND IN A MANNER THAT ACTUALLY KEEPS THE QUEST TO IMPROVE YOUR GOLF SWING ON A SIMPLE AND THEREFORE WORKABLE CONCEPTUAL LEVEL. There is nothing new to this statement. Just about every good golf teacher worth his or her salt advocates the proper and effective use of the large muscles of the body to control the swing and serve as the source of power for the swing. But the emphasis is different under the Hip to Hip Method, particularly when looking at how the backswing and its sequence of motion occurs, and how the method can be used to actually create tempo.

And, let's face it. Unless you are a tour professional, a teenager or collegiate golfer who is playing 3-5 times per week, hitting a lot of range balls and getting in some quality putting time, you just don't have the time to keep a highly complicated golf swing, or a golf swing that is unorthodox or peculiar, performing at a solid level. It does not matter what your level of ability is, and does not matter whether your handicap is a 25, a 15, a 1 or a plus 3. If you are an adult who has a job, your only opportunity to learn how to improve is late afternoons and whatever weekend time you can take away from your family. Learning a lot of intricate details about golf swing mechanics is at best an uphill task, and leads to paralysis through analysis. So we need to find one or two master moves that have a lot of room in which to improve instead of trying to learn and master 15 moving parts of a golf swing that may or may not be fundamentally essential. So let's try a method of swinging the golf club that is focused on the truly big picture.

So, okay, what is my golf theory? It is very simple. THE GOLF SWING, WHICH TENDS TO WORK BEST IS THE GOLF SWING THAT TENDS TO, OVER TIME, BE DRIVEN BY AND DOMINATED BY THE HIPS MORE AND MORE AS THE PLAYER IMPROVES.

The better you move your hips, the more authoritatively your HIPS CAN GOVERN and CONTROL what the rest of your body, the rest of the moving parts of your golf swing, do during the swing. The rest of the body is the work force and lower management. But you hips are top management, even your golf swing's CEO. That is what golf swing leadership is all about. From start to finish, the hips control everything else, including tempo. Period.

Think about the simplicity of focusing on your hips as a learning issue. If the hips can be used to drive the rest of the swing, if the hips can serve as the stabilizing force of your swing and insure dynamic balance, if the hips can control tempo and timing, and control swing plane and control the speed and power of your downswing, then you can remove the mechanical clutter from your attempts at golf swing mechanical improvement and instead focus on getting one set of athletic movements to work better and better and better. And believe me, for most all golfers other than top college players and touring pros, there is tremendous potential for improvement in hip turn.

Before we start, you should be aware of my caveat about expected results. The Hip to Hip Method is not a quick fix. And it is not by any stretch of the imagination any type of panacea. Mastering first class hip movement in a golf swing cannot be learned in a couple of practice sessions, a few weeks, over the course of a full season or even in a year. In my estimation, achieving first rate hip movement during the golf swing takes years to develop. It is much like the snow skier's quest to improve one simple athletic move as he or she progresses from beginner to novice to intermediate to highly skilled to expert, the shift in balance from one ski to another as the years go by and the slopes become ever more steeper and challenging. But the real dividend comes from focusing on one set of movements to improve the other moving parts of your swing.

Moreover, by focusing on one set of moves, you will have the ability to keep coming back to one set of principles with a highly focused mental effort without getting sidetracked on hot tips and fads. Keeping your learning and skill focus centered on one set of goals for improvement is what is most needed when you are not playing this wonderful game on a day in and day out basis. The less time you have to play, the more important it becomes to keep your striving to improve focused on one set of golf swing skills. An it is my view that if you can learn to get your hips moving in the right direction, you will have a very good chance of causing the other moving parts of your golf swing to follow along.

THE HIPS MUST START THE SWING

The first principle in the Hip to Hip Method is that THE WINDING OF THE HIPS MUST BE THE FIRST MOVE IN THE BACKSWING. Why? There are several reasons. First, by getting your hips into the act from the very beginning, you will almost assuredly keep your hips moving throughout the backswing so that they fully wind up, thereby increasing the chances that they continue moving on the way back through, during the downswing. And why is this so important? It is because the name of the game in a good, solid golf swing that delivers the clubhead into the back of the ball is in making sure the hips beat the arms and hands through the impact zone.

The hips must move faster than the shoulders, arms and hands through the impact zone for several reasons. The key generator of power in a golf swing is the rapid, swift and certain rotation and clearing of the hips through impact. It is this rotational power from the inside out, from the very inner core of your body, somewhere in your spine around your waist that is the center of gravity, or the hub of the wheel, that creates the centrifugal force. This inside out, centrifugal force from your trunkline or waist is the base from which the whiplash effect or leveraging effect of the rest of your moving swing parts derives energy. From the inside out, starting with your hips, the downswing unfolds with your shoulders unwinding, causing your arms to swing out and into the back of the ball at the impact zone, and causing your clubhead to be unleashed from the cock of your wrists.

In addition to the rotational power driven by your hips, your hips must simply clear out of the way at impact to give your arms a chance to unleash the clubhead into the back of the ball without your right hand and wrist rolling over your left hand and wrist, which will cause a hook with better players and a slice with higher handicappers who also throw the clubhead outside of the ball's target line by beginning the downswing with their right hand coming over their right foot where all the weight is.

Another reason the hips should initiate the swing is that the circular sweeping of the clubhead and clubshaft back and away from the ball will very, very likely be on the right swing plane if the arms and hands have not artificially caused any alteration away from the natural swing plane that will result when the arms follow rather than lead the hips away from the ball.

A third reason, which may be the most important of all, is tempo. If you simply try the experiment of standing at address in your own living room and try taking the club away by using only the winding rotation of your hips to move the clubhead away from the ball, you will immediately sense, and realize for sure, that you simply cannot take the clubhead away very fast at all. In fact it is almost impossible to jerk the clubhead back away from the ball, and it is by definition not going to be an overly quick takeaway with your hands and arms—they are not moving! So many players bemoan how much they have to fight being "too quick" during the takeaway, which thereby destroys a smooth tempo that gradually builds up to powerful speed in the second .75 seconds of the golf swing rather than the first .75 seconds. Taking the clubhead back with a simple rotation of the hips will unquestionably slow your backswing down to the point it needs to go.

The subject of tempo leads to another interesting question— how slow should your golf swing be to have good tempo? My view is that good tempo and good swing mechanical sequence go hand in hand. I believe you can freely swing a golf club just as fast as you are able with one critical caveat—the circular movement of the hands and arms along the arc of the swing at any point during the swing until past impact, should never outrace the rotational position of the hips. As long as the hands and arms follow behind the hips at every stage of the golf swing until impact, your swing speed is not relevant.

Of course, this seems to beg the question, how can you make sure your arms and hands do not outrace your hip rotation going back and going back through into the back of the ball? One way to try to do it is by trying to slow down the motion of your arms and hands during takeaway and backswing. This is usually referred to as "swinging within myself" or "not swinging so hard at the ball" or having a slow, smooth tempo. But in my view slowing the arms and hands down by focusing on their speed is much too hard of a task to pull off! From one day to the next, your metabolism changes, and your biorhythms fluctuate so that you are totally relaxed one day and hyper the next. The speed with which you do things varies from day to day, and this is especially true of your day to day tempo in golf. It is also on some days just too hard to have enough feedback as to whether you are "too slow" or "too fast," so you cannot really use how you feel from one day to the next as a reliable measure of how fast or slow you are swinging the golf club.

But if you start out your swing by moving the hips first, then your arms can simply "catch up" eventually, at the right moment, which is impact. Until impact, there is no real need for the arms and hands to have caught up with the rotational leadership of the hips. So, the sooner you can get your hips into the pivotal lead of your golf swing, the better.

THE MASTER SEQUENCE

The second critical component of the Hip to Hip Method is that the sequence of movement always follows this order: HIPS EXCLUSIVELY FIRST, THEN SHOULDERS EXCLUSIVELY SECOND, THEN VIRTUALLY AUTOMATICALLY ARMS, HANDS AND WRISTS. This order is followed both during the backswing and the downswing. During the backswing, the takeaway is initiated with the hips AND THE HIPS ONLY. Once the hips have almost finished their winding during the backswing, the shoulders, which have automatically turned 30-40 degrees during the backswing once the hips have turned away, AS A DIRECT RESULT OF BEING CONNECTED TO YOUR HIPS, will complete their turn, which is essentially a turning or tightening of the left shoulder under your chin. And, once the hips and shoulders have finished their wind up, the hands can finish the backswing with a folding of the right elbow and forearm coupled with whatever wrist cock results from the inertial movement of the clubhead as it is being swung over the top of your right shoulder at the top of the backswing.

On the downswing, the same sequence occurs. First the left hip swings around vigorously toward the target as your weight shifts back onto your left foot, and as it is rapidly rotating back through the impact zone, the shoulders, being pulled around toward the target to a large extent simply being connected biomechanically to the hips, continues around, which by centrifugal force slings the arms, hands and clubhead around and out toward the back of the golf ball down the target line.

The master sequence again is very simple: Hips turn back first, then shoulders turn back, then arms and wrists fold up, then hips turn first back to the target, then, when cleared past the target, the shoulders, arms and hands are unleashed through the impact zone. The trick to using this sequence, especially during the backswing, is to wait on your hips to finish, almost coming to a full "stop" in winding up, before you start finishing the turn of your shoulders with whatever turn they have left, and that you don't move your arms or hands at all during the backswing under their own power and with their own shoulder, arm and hand muscles, until the wind of the shoulders has also stopped. Illustations 4.1A and 4.1B demonstrate how the hips have already finished their work at the beginning of the backswing, leaving only the shoulders and arms to move during the last half of the backswing.

Is the so called master sequence sound fundamentally? If it is based on what the swings of great golfers look like, the answer is a resounding yes. But words and deed in golf instruction, even among the greats, do not always match up. Consider some of the history and rhetoric.

In *The Fundamentals of Hogan*, David Ledbetter noted that Hogan viewed his pre swing waggle as related to Hogan's theory that the swing was a chain reaction. Ledbetter said, "During the backswing, the hands moved first, followed by the arms, shoulder and lower body. The order was then reversed on the downswing—lower body, shoulders, arms and hands. This sequence was critical, according to Hogan, and the golfer who accomplished it could strike a ball with tremendous force." I totally agree with Hogan's and Ledbetter's statement of sequence for the downswing. In fact, I would go so far as saying that Ben Hogan should be credited with stating the most important fundamental in golf when he claimed that the downswing must be initiated with the hips. But their statement about the sequence of hands first, then shoulders, then hips is suspect. First, if you actually look at swing sequence photographs of Ben Hogan during the backswing, it sure looks as though he has achieved a relatively flat swing plane on his backswing, which I submit can be achieved only with the use of a large rotational motion with the hips during the backswing.

On page 48 of *The Fundamentals of Hogan,* the lower right photo of Hogan at the top of his swing shows that he clearly and without any doubt has made a huge turn of the hips going back.

Ill. 4.1A—The gap between the knees shows the hips have finished winding halfway into the backswing.

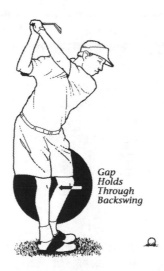

**Gap
Holds
Through
Backswing**

Ill. 4.1B—Only the shoulders and arms are moving during the last part of the backswing.

In fact, Hogan's belt buckle has turned to the point that it is almost facing the camera from a rear view angle photographing Hogan down the target line. This degree of hip wind and turn on Hogan's backswing is almost as full as his clearing of hips at impact, where the belt buckle is facing down the target line. While Hogan may have felt his hands moved first during the backswing, it is most clear that his hips moved as much or more, and, I would submit, Hogan's hips beat his arms to the top of his backswing. While Hogan may have indeed moved his arms and hands first away from the ball, his hips caught up and eventually got into the lead role, not just during the downswing, but also during his backswing.

Even if assuming for the sake of argument that Hogan did in fact and did believe that the arms and hands started the backswing, Bobby Jones most assuredly did not. In *Bobby Jones on Golf*, the 1997 revised edition by Sidney L. Matthew, Jones was quoted in his thoughts about how the backswing started and unfolded. Bobby Jones said, "The first movement after the waggle is completed should be a quick and very slight turn of the hips in the direction of the hole, the right knee flexing slightly toward the ball and the left leg straightening at the same time. The almost imperceptible motion is transmitted through the arms and hands, but it does not originate with them. The purpose of the press is to throw the hips and legs into position [emphasis added] *to start the swing*. The next movement is the real start of the backswing and here again the hips and legs supply the motive force, the hands for a time simply *FOLLOWING THE LEAD*. This is the 'drag' we hear so much about. The hips turn away from the ball and the hands and arms do not move until they are literally pulled away by the left."

In a later part of his book, Jones includes a section entitled "The Backswing—A Most Important Part of the Game" that has the subtitle, "Hip Motion Comes First" Jones is quoted as saying, "That the first motion of the backswing should be made by the legs or hips there can be little doubt. To start it with the hands results inevitably in the lifting upright motion characteristic of the beginner who swing the club as though it were an ax, elevating it to the shoulder position without a semblance of the weight shift and shoulder turn effected by the professional."

Tiger Woods also pays careful attention to the turning of his hips during the backswing as well. In his instructional book, *How I Play Golf,* Tiger discusses the sequence of motion during his backswing. He says, "The sequence of motion on the backswing is the same for the driver as for every other club. But I do pay special attention to my hips. I make absolutely sure that my hips turn rather than slide to my right. Turning the hips is one of the first signs I'm accumulating power. This rotary motion in my hips and shoulders is much like loading a giant spring. By the time I reach the top, my hips and shoulders are primed to unload with tremendous speed."

Notice that Tiger's sensations are that his hip turn is one of the *first* signs he is accumulating power. It is telling to observe that when Tiger discusses the accumulation of power during his backswing, he does not mention his arms and hands, and neither does he say anything about trying to restrict his hips. Indeed, he is stressing the turn of his hips in a rotary fashion as though he were winding a giant spring. Thus, both Tiger and Bobby Jones espouse the dominant roles the hips play during the backswing.

I am not advocating that the arms, hands, clubshaft and clubhead have to play a totally passive role, totally like a rag doll, as the backswing begins or progresses. Obviously, the arms and club do turn back away from the ball as a part of the backswing. Indeed, I fully recognize that a so-called "one piece takeaway" is a fundamentally valid method to start the backswing. But I maintain that the initial backswing motion of the arms, hands and club can be fully in response to the domination and lead of the hips and shoulders in turning away from the ball and that originating the motion of the backswing with your hips is in no sense inconsistent with a "one piece takeaway." I also believe you will not in any way undermine your backswing by letting your arms and hands be even more passive to the point that there is some lag in you clubhead as a result of the hip domination from the start. The lag type takeaway tends to promote more relaxation in your arms and shoulders as the backswing begins.

Now that we have reviewed the big picture, let's take a look at exactly how you can get to work on moving your hips correctly.

THE HIP DRAW BACKSWING: THE FIRST MASTER MOVE

The first master move in your backswing under the Hip to Hip Method is what I refer to as the "the hip draw." When you begin to think about turning your hips during the backswing, the issue becomes one of how? How do the hips turn in a windup fashion during the backswing? Does the left hip and right hip turn together, as if in a barrel, or is there something else to consider?

If you consider the skeletal make up of your spine, shoulder bones, and hips, it becomes apparent that the hips do not really "turn" in any kind of a lateral circular motion. Why? Because the spine is tilted at approximately 30 degrees and the hips must rotate in complete congruence with your spine angle. This means that what is described as a turn of the hips away from the ball during the backswing is not actually a horizontal turn parallel to the ground, but a drawing of the right hip straight back from its position at address. If the left hip and right hip simply rotated in a flat circular plane in a plane parallel to the ground, your spine would actually be moved out of position, causing you to actually sway away from the ball, and perhaps actually lift up and move your upper body totally out of position.

This drawing of the right hip makes geometric sense because the angle of your spine during the backswing and your right thigh operates more like a hinge that compresses as the spine properly rotates along its 30 degree incline. Thus the drawing of the right hip in a rearward motion will actually cause the hips to rotate on a plane that is consistent with and in stabilization of the tilted rotation of your spine.

The Drawing of the Right Hip

As you begin your backswing with the draw of your right hip, what is the sensation you will feel? Let's focus for a moment on the movement itself, and then describe some of the sensations you may feel as this motion begins to be learned.

The Hip Draw Movement

The draw of the right hip rearward, straight back from the target line will actually cause the hips to rotate on a rotational plane that is consistent with the tilt of your spine during the backswing. One way you can tell this movement is occurring correctly is when the angle between your right thigh and the right side of your torso becomes sharper. I call this "compressing your angle." This compression of your angle will actually accomplish two key moves in your backswing. First it will insure that your hips are winding on a swing plane that is in complete harmony with the rotational movement of your spine. Second, it will actually help you maintain your spine angle and stabilize your upper body during the backswing in several important respects.

If you are "compressing your angle," you cannot simultaneously lift your head or sway your upper body off center because the rearward movement of the right hip won't let it. Compressing your angle by definition means that you have kept your spine angle steady over the ball and have not therefore moved off the ball. Third, the draw of the right hip insures that the left hip follows along its prescribed pathway, in an almost passive manner, taking its cue and lead from the motion of the right hip.

The use of the right hip as the leading player in this drama of a hip dominated swing is not new. In his instructional book, *My Golden Lessons,* Jack Nicklaus carefully described how he always focused on turning his right hip back to wind his hips during the backswing. He also advocates using reference to the right hip on the downswing. The Hip to Hip Method, however, focuses on clearing the left hip during the downswing as the primary motivator of hip action back to the ball.

What are some of the feels or sensations you can expect as you begin your backswing with a rearward draw of your right hip? One of the images I have had as the right hip is drawn to the rear is that I am cranking a lawnmower with my right hip. Imagine at the beginning of your backswing that you are pulling the cord out from the lawnmower with your right hand in a forceful, pulling action accompanied by a pulling back of your right hip. It is the same with the draw of the right hip, except you are not pulling anything during the backswing with your right hand. But you can essentially "feel" the right hip drawing or "cranking" back in this manner. The draw of the right hip is not quick or jerky, but gradual and certain.

Another key sensation you will feel is you right buttocks steadily jutting out from behind you, as an increase in pressure is felt on your right hip. You feel as though some extra weight is being loaded up on your right hip as it juts out behind you and begins to feel stretched almost as if you are a weight lifter in a clean and jerk lift after the clean, squatting with a lot of weight bearing down on your hips. Some teachers and players call this "loading your right hip." See Illustration 4.2.

Another imaginary concept or feeling you may sense or wish to use as a concentration technique, instead of sensing your right hip "drawing" away from the target line, is the feeling that your backswing is started by a clockwise rotational windup of your belly button around in front of you and to your right as your belly button tries to wind up over your right heel (another key balancing factor discussed below). See Illustration 4.3. This is another sensation that can help you achieve the right kind of hip wind up rotation that is consistent with the rotational winding of your spine. This alternative sensation is equally effective in fully winding your hips during the backswing to create the level of coil needed to make a full turn.

You may want to experiment with both the right hip "draw" and the belly button rotation over the right heel during some practice sessions to learn which technique makes more sense to you personally. Either concept will work, but you may find that one way to wind up your hips is easier to feel or repeat than the other. The important point is that you use whatever move feels most comfortable to you while winding the hips up as fully as possible over your right heel.

As you begin to feel your right hip being loaded up as the right hip draws straight away from the target line, or your belly button is turning away from the target toward your right heel, another key sensation should be an ever increasing pressure of weight onto your right heel. And critically, that is exactly where your weight should be going during your backswing. Instructors over the years have indeed stressed keeping your balance by playing "within your feet" and making sure you shift your weight into your right foot while keeping that weight from going past the inside or instep of the right foot. The problem with the right foot instep concept is that it acts as little more than a set of "brakes" against a lateral movement of your weight onto your right foot, which would result in swaying off the ball if not restrained by your brake. The clear implication is that the weight shift should be lateral, but the problem is that a lateral shift of weight from both feet primarily to the right foot does not promote any type of energetic hip turn.

Ill. 4.2—Drawing or leading your right hip to start the backswing.

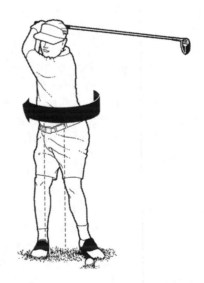

Ill. 4.3—Winding your belly button over your right heel.

Instead of fighting to keep your weight on the inside of your right foot during the backswing using a lateral shift of weight from left to right, try loading as much weight onto your right heel throughout the backswing as your right hip draws straight away from the target line and your belt buckle turns or rotates back to the point of being positioned over your right foot. This will insure that your weight does not sway to the outside of your right foot, but it will simultaneously and strongly encourage your hips to undertake their critical winding and turning function as the backswing progresses. In *How I Play Golf,* Tiger Woods leaves no doubt how he shifts his weight during his backswing. In describing one of his six keys to a great backswing, he says, "My weight is gathered onto my right heel." Moving your weight onto your right heel as your right hip draws back will insure great balance while providing the ever so critical windup or coil of the hips needed to generate power for the downswing.

THE SECOND MASTER MOVE:
DELAYED SHOULDERS AND ARMS

The second master move is that the shoulders and arms delay active involvement until the hips have virtually completed their windup in the backswing. This does not mean that the arms and shoulders do not move during the first part of the backswing. Indeed they do in a big way. But the muscles of the shoulders, arms and hands allow the hips to lead the backswing until the hips can no longer lead because the turn of the hips is complete. What I am saying is that you use your hips and your hips only to drive the backswing with the Hip to Hip Method until they stop turning. Then and only then will you use your shoulders to finish out their turn, and then and only then will you use your arms and hands to complete your backswing with what is essentially a minor amount of effort needed to simply finish folding your right arm softly into position and a relaxed cock of the wrists that is caused more by the weight of the clubshaft and clubhead pulling the wrists cocked at the top of the backswing rather than the wrists doing much work.

Let's take a closer look at how you can implement this so called second master move and how a good backswing unfolds as a result of using this sequence. When your backswing is initiated or started with an active draw of the right hip back away from the target, or ball line of flight line, with the arms and shoulders relaxed and not doing any work in the beginning, the hip rotation that you create will automatically begin to draw your shoulders into a turning motion simply because the hips are rotating your spine, which in turn is causing your shoulders to rotate. If the right hip draws back fully, then the hips have turned about 50-60 degrees and the shoulder have automatically turned to that degree since your spine has essentially turned that much, too.

Because your hands are bound together to the golf club by gripping it, the rotation of the right shoulder generated by your "hip draw turn" automatically begins to pull the clubshaft away from the ball. Your arms will passively follow the lead of your hip draw and the consequential shoulder turn just fine, and will not require any muscle movement of the forearms or hands whatsoever. The draw of the right hip back away from the line of flight and the resulting shoulder turn that goes along with it will provide enough backswing motion to cause your hands, and the clubshaft and clubhead, to get to a point in relation to your body that is about waist high, or half the way through your backswing.

The real beauty of the Hip to Hip Method takeaway is that you will start the clubshaft and clubhead back away from the ball on the perfect swing plane in a low wide arc without any involvement of your arms and hands! All of the instructional ideas you have ever accumulated about the takeaway concerning your hands, how the clubhead should be taken away from the ball, or how you should cock your wrists, can be discarded! Until your hands are waist high, you can simply let them relax and enjoy being taken along for the ride! You will begin to learn that you can literally and totally trust your hips to complete your takeaway of the clubhead and your arms without any help at all from your hand and arms!

Once the hips have finished their critical business of initiating the backswing and completing close to one half of the arc of your arm backswing, its time to finish out your backswing. How do you do it? You finish it out, first by finishing your shoulder turn. Although the hips have moved about 50-60 degrees, the shoulders can, if you have sufficient muscular flexibility (an assumption that is not always true, and a very key issue about swing length that we will consider in much more detail later), turn another 30-40 degrees, so that at the top of your backswing, your shoulders, with the key assistance of your hips first, and then on their own, have turned somewhere between 90-100 degrees in all (note the 100 degrees is for collegiate golfers and all sorts of very supple and strong younger players, to whom middle aged hackers and seniors commonly refer as "limberbacks").

So do it! Finish your shoulder turn out by turning your left shoulder underneath your chin as much as you can. This will have three key effects. First it will maximize the amount of shoulder turn you can make to store up the kind of power you will need to unleash the clubhead in the most efficient and forceful, thought controlled, manner into the back of the golf ball. Second, it will greatly calm your arms and hands down during the backswing by keeping them out of the backswing act as long as possible. Third, the additional rotation of your shoulders will continue moving your arms and hands, and the clubshaft and clubhead, around the arc of your backswing to the point that the clubhead is swinging over your right shoulder, past your hands, as if it were being "slung" around you to the top of your backswing.

The result of this slinging motion is that the clubhead's inertia begins to pull your arms and hands tight, and actually begins the cock of your wrists without any active motion of your wrists. By keeping your arms and wrists relaxed until this point, you allow the clubhead to travel along the swing path it naturally wants to follow without any artificial manipulation of your hands and wrists. Artificial manipulation or cocking of your hands or wrists too early during the backswing can ruin your swing plane and create timing and tempo problems from which you can never recover.

At this point your backswing is almost done. Your hips have fully coiled and your shoulders have turned as far as they can. As your clubshaft nears parallel with the gravity of your clubhead and clubshaft pulling your arms and hands into position and causing your wrists to cock, you can now feel free to let your arms and hands finish out your swing. How? It is really so much of a small type of motion that you will begin to wonder why your arms and hands ever played such a major role in your prior swing. The motion feels almost like a tiny, but soft, flick of the wrists to finish off what feels like the last ½ of your wrist cock, together with a relaxed and a small amount of unhurried folding of your right forearm. That's it! Your backswing is done. See how simple it all sounds.

I must warn you again that this type of backswing is much easier said than done. You may have accumulated years and years of tense or aggressive arm and hand movements during your backswing that will not go away easily. You may have been initiating your backswing with an early aggressive wrist cock. You may have aggressively jerked the clubhead back abruptly, and without realizing it, picked up your club going back, using the arms to create a type of lifting motion that undermines a full turn of your torso and shoulders and undercuts your attempts to build real "coil." Whatever problems you may have in the way of overactive arms and hands during the backswing will not vanish in your first attempts to swing using the Hip to Hip Method, nor will they vanish overnight or in the course of a week or two. The Hip to Hip Method will definitely lead to significant improvements in your swing and ball striking ability in due course, but it will take time, patience and a fair amount of effort to relearn the sequence of muscular motion that allows the hips to drive first, then the shoulders to finish turning, then the arms to take the last minor role of what is really nothing more than completing the cock of your wrists.

Is the Hip to Hip backswing really that simple? Well, yes and no. The sequence of movement—hips, then shoulders, then arms, hands and wrists—is obviously simple enough for any of us to remember. But the golf swing is not simply some kind of intellectual exercise. The motor skills and muscle memory needed to swing this way will take quite a bit of time to develop, and these skills will not, I can assure you, come overnight. But the simplicity of the method is that until you get your hips moving back right with the right hip draw, until you get your weight on your backswing onto your right heel, until you make your arms wait for your hips and shoulders to do their work, you have a lot of progress to make, but at least you know where you are going in terms of learning goals. These moves are not very complicated, but they are challenging to learn fully and master to the point you can totally stop having to even think about them. But at least you have a blueprint, or a plan of action that, if embraced and accomplished, can move you forward as you get better at the Hip to Hip Method, not one step forward and two back.

Best of all, you are freed from having to hunt down some magic secret to swinging a golf club, and you are freed from having to clutter your mind with a truckload of superfluous, unfundamental "swing tips" and fads to find your golf swing. You begin to understand, and feel the key fundamental of golf at work in your swing, which is the better you can rotate your hips going back, the better your can unwind them and clear them out of the way going through, and the better you will be able to hit good solid golf shots.

This approach to golf swing learning is far superior than flailing away in a perpetual state of confusion by jumping around from swing tip to swing tip, method to method in a futile search for the holy grail. The Hip to Hip Method also recognizes that there is no holy grail in swinging a golf club. Once you address the ball with good posture, alignment, and setup, there are only three fundamental motions your body can make, the turning of its hips, the turning of its shoulders and the movement of its arms and hands. As Ben Hogan, Jack Nicklaus, Tiger Woods and Bobby Jones actually swung a club, and at least as Bobby Jones expressly understood, the biggest fundamental moves of all are with your hips.

THE HIP SNAP DOWNSWING:
THE THIRD MASTER MOVE

It is obviously important to make a backswing that winds your swing up correctly, building power and positioning you to make the best pass you can at the golf ball during the downswing. But the most important moves of all are the ones your hips make to decisively shift from your backswing to your downswing, and to rotate and clear out of the way as your arms, hands and clubhead passes through the impact zone. I refer to this third master move under the Hip to Hip Method as the "Hip Snap Downswing." Your downswing will happen in about 1/3 to 1/2 of a second, so you have little or no time to think your way through it. You can only capture sensations to know whether you may be doing it right. But there is definitely a right way to move your hips during the downswing, and fortunately, you can improve the performance of your hip rotation during the downswing with some good drills and some hard won practice.

The Snap: Throwing the Left Hip Back

Okay, so you have made a great backswing, with your right hip drawing back, loading up your right hip and shifting most

(70-80 percent) of your weight at the top of your backswing into your right heel. Now what? Well, if you are like many high handicappers, the first move you make down is a throwing action of your hands and arms toward the ball in a manner that is out and over the line of flight and outside your ball's intended target line. And, if you do this while staying stuck on your right foot, the out and over move will be extreme, and you will be hitting severe slices or smothered hooks. Or, if you have enough balance and skill to be able to get your weight during the beginning of your downswing quickly back onto your left foot, you may be prone to hitting pushes or swooping hooks as your right wrist rolls over your left in a desperate attempt to square up the clubface into the back of the ball. If you don't square the face up, a huge push or worse, push slice, can occur.

So, what is the solution to this parade of horribles? As Hogan clearly understood and stated, "THE HIPS MUST GO FIRST." Unless you train yourself to have your hips drive your downswing, you can never really expect to play to your full potential as a ball striker. So okay, how do you do it? Before we work on how to do it, let's take a moment to fully understand what the hips actually accomplish in helping you hit straight, powerful and flush golf shots.

What Happens in Clearing or Unwinding the Hips?

When you reach the top of your backswing correctly, your hips are coiled up together with your shoulders and arms, poised to unleash a huge amount of power into the back of the golf ball. With the drive and lead of your left hip from the top of your swing, a chain reaction happens. First, the left hip simultaneously turns forcefully back to the target and shifts your entire lower torso and weight laterally back onto your left foot. This causes a very strong pulling of your torso with torque and rotational force, which in turn twists and begins to unwind your shoulders and arms back toward the ball.

In *Classic Instruction*, by Bobby Jones and Ben Crenshaw, Jones, commenting on the start of his downswing, says, "The hips lead as the unwinding begins, and by pulling against the hands and the weight of the club, draw the left arm taut."

The counter force caused by this very rapid and forceful unwinding of the left hip is much like the reverse cranking of wet soggy clothes in a washing machine as the spindle reverse shifts in the opposite direction as the clothes are rotating in the other direction. The physical result is a cranking of the shoulders, arms, clubshaft and clubhead in a similar manner so that the torque power thrown out to your clubshaft is actually at this millisecond dramatically increased, and in accomplished players, this wrenching transition will very often result in an increase in the cock of your wrists naturally, delivering the shaft into the impact zone with a tremendous amount of pent up force.

The second thing that happens physically is that the quick and forceful shift of your hips and weight toward the target pulls your arms downward into a lower swing plane, inside the line of flight, so that the clubhead can be delivered from inside the target line into the back of the ball. The third thing that happens if your hips are rapidly unwinding, rotating and clearing past the impact zone is that the clearing of your hips rather than the rotation or rolling of your wrists is the force that squares up your clubface as it crushes into the back of the golf ball at impact.

Using the hips to square up the clubface at impact is an extremely critical concept. Great players do this consistently, and players of lesser ability do not. If there is any such thing as a real "secret" of the golf swing, squaring up the clubface at impact with the hips is it. If you rely on your hands and wrists to square the clubface at impact, you better have perfect timing because a millisecond of miss too slow or too fast will not square the clubface and a poor, offline shot will result. But who has perfect timing? Nobody does, and to rely heavily on timing invites erratic golf. In contrast, to rely on the hips to square up the clubface at impact takes the tiny muscles of the hands and wrists out of it, greatly reducing the timing factor of your hands as the arbiter of a square clubface. So back to the issue at hand—how do I make my hips work?

A Hip Turn or Hip Snap?

There is no doubt that a rotation of your left hip back to the target occurs when your backswing begins in the right fashion. But to achieve such a rapid turn, while at the same time instantaneously and simultaneously shifting your weight back onto your left leg and foot, takes some real doing. It is an athletic move that must happen so unbelievably quickly that you don't really have time to think at all about rotating hips and shifting weight. So what is a technique you can use to get that huge, intense sequence of events happen in all of ½ of a second? My recommendation is that you conceptualize this rapid turning of the left hip and accompanying shift of your body weight onto your left foot as a hip "snap."

How the Hip Snap Works

Okay, so in order to get your hips moving extremely rapidly and forcefully to initiate the downswing, to rotate and unwind powerfully to transmit the release of power of the clubhead with great centrifugal force, and to clear them out of the way to allow your arms and hands to pass by impact without rolling over, all in ½ of a second, you have to pull all of it off with one fell swoop. What is the trick? In my honest opinion, there actually is a trick to make your hips do it all in a flash, and trying to think about turning them back to the target is just not powerful enough, and just not quick enough. We've got to employ some type of device that, like the spaceships in Star Wars, will propel us into "hyperspace." And the trick is the "Hip Snap"

The hip snap concept is that you are getting your left hip out of the way so fast during your downswing that, in one flash move, BAM! It is gone . . . . out of there . . . . now your see it and now you don't. Recall in the beginning of this book where we looked at many of the game's great players and discovered that at impact their left hip has cleared way out of the way, with the left leg straightened, most all of the golfer's weight onto his or her right foot and the belt buckle facing the target. Think about it. You have ½ second to do it. So we better be not just quick, but explosive. How can we explode our left hip out of the way so rapidly? I think it is by snapping the left hip back out of the way. You have to feel as though you are literally shooting it out of the way!

The Forty-Five Degree Concept

The most effective technique to snap your left hip out of the way so quickly while shifting your weight onto your left foot just as quickly is to throw it where it belongs at impact. And from a running start, with your left hip wound up at the top of your backswing and pointing somewhat toward the golf ball, it has to at least feel that it is traveling FROM THAT POSITION, and with great speed and force, in a somewhat straight line at a 45 degree angle to the center of your stance or the ball, toward and then past, your left heel. And at the same time your left leg snaps straight. That is the feeling you will get when trying this trick. Illustrations 4.4A and 4.4B show how the left hip "snaps" or clears out at impact as the left leg posts up and the player's weight is strongly shifted down and onto the left foot.

Why the Hip Snap Sensation is Actually a Turn

In reality, your hips will actually rotate and unwind in a circular pattern, just like they are supposed to. The snap of the left hip, back to an imaginary position 45 degrees behind you may feel like a snap but never mind. This 45 degree snap of the left hip back over and beyond your left heel will actually cause your left hip to rotate rapidly out of the way, clearing out of the impact zone, while at the same time shifting your body weight onto your left foot. If your skill level is at the point of already having a good solid weight shift at the beginning of your downswing onto your left foot, you may benefit with the sensation of actually snapping your left hip straight back from the target line at a 90 degree angle back over your left heel. But the trick is to get that left hip out of the way as quickly and cleanly as possible as the dominant driver of your downswing. Illustration 4.5 provides a rear view of the left hip rotating out of the way for a right handed golfer.

Wrenching of the Waist

When you aggressively unwind your left hip back to the target while forcefully shifting your weight onto your left foot, your entire torso is twisting rapidly, leaving your shoulders, arms and hands behind, but only for an instant. They catch up extremely rapidly as the centrifugal force of your downswing unleashes into your arms and the clubshaft, releasing all of the stored up energy produced by the hip driven torque between your hips and chest, or in short your waist. As you begin to start your downswing by driving the rotation and shifting of your hips, this indeed may start to feel like a wrenching motion. It is quite different from the heaving or lurching movement that you may have made in the past because of your tendency to try attacking the ball from the top of your backswing with your hands and arms. If you begin to feel this violent wrenching, celebrate! You are on your way to developing a hip driven downswing.

Straightening or Posting of the Left Leg

Another goal of the Hip to Hip downswing is posting or straightening your left leg. As your left hip rotates over your left foot, your left leg should straighten up which accelerates your hip spin through the impact zone and provides a brace against which to release all of the torque and centrifugal energy into the back of the ball. This is critical to a strong and reliable hip spin through the ball and it allows your left hip to clear out of the way at impact to allow your arms to pass into the back of the ball and through impact unimpeded.

Ill. 4.4A—The hip "snap" and the 45° concept.

Ill. 4.4B—Hip "snap" from a front view. Moving the left hip out of the way squares the club face.

Ill. 4.5—Clearing out the left hip at impact

If instead you allow the hips to slide toward the target at impact due to a sagging or overly flexed left knee, you will not completely turn your left hip out of the way and your arms and wrists cannot unleash into the back of the golf ball without the right forearm and right wrist rolling over your left forearm and wrist. I call this rollover and its effect on the clubhead at impact is disastrous. The outcome from a failure to fully spin your hips ahead of your arms through impact and clear them out of the way with the imperative use of a straightened left leg is rollover much like the rollover of a car in a bad wreck, except that instead of injuries and fatalities, you get smothered hooks or severe slices.

Shifting Weight to the Left Foot

As indicated above, it is essential that as the left hip spins aggressively counter clockwise back to the target line and then past it, clearing out of the way to the left of your left foot, your entire body weight must get back to your left foot. Hip spin without the weight shift is not sufficient, and will result in your casting the club totally over the target line in an outside in swing path that will cause a severe slice if you do close up your clubface or a bad pull if you do. You must get your weight onto your left foot as soon as possible from the top of your backswing, period. Later in this book are several balancing drills that will help you master weight shift. If you have difficulty doing this, I suggest you focus on your inability to shift your weight immediately and aggressively, because without it your golf swing just will not work.

Impact Balance and Down and Though the Ball

Using the Hip Snap technique to achieve good hip spin during your downswing will also require you to have what I call strong "top heavy" balance, too. Top heavy balance is your ability to stay centered over the ball at impact with your upper body. This means that you keep yourself from "coming out of the shot" and raising up your upper torso too quick at or immediately following impact. You must stay "down and through" the shot.

Staying down with the ball is extremely critical. But with an aggressive unwinding of your hips during the downswing, the temptation is to clear out of the way at impact not only with your hips but your upper torso, too. The trick is to keep your upper body and spine centered over the ball in a calm still manner at impact as the left hip aggressively completes its task of clearing and spinning out of the way, and of getting out of the way of your arms. Both must happen but it is not easy to pull off, particularly if you are a middle aged or senior golfer. Why? A great part of the reason is flexibility. Unless your lateral muscles running down your left side are sufficiently stretched out and relaxed, aggressively clearing your left hip out of the way at impact while staying down and covering the ball is simply too hard. The only good way you can avoid a failure to stay down and through the ball is to work on some key flexibility exercises.

Why the Downswing Hip Snap Beats Other Concepts

The left hip "snap," whereby the left hip snaps at what SEEMS like a 45 degree angle from the golf ball, while the left leg straightens and your weight is thrown onto your left foot, in my opinion, beats other ideas and concepts about the downswing. It is not that I disagree with some of the teaching principles about pulling the club down with your left hand, or getting your right elbow into your side at the start of the downswing. But in my estimation, these ideas don't quite present, in an integrated or unified manner, what you should be trying to achieve with your downswing. THE master move on the downswing is a strong, but precise move that will take the torque power stored up at the top of your backswing and immediately get your left hip to where it absolutely must be to achieve a solid impact—CLEARED OUT OF THE WAY. The ability to pull this off in one fell swoop, instantaneously, and without any hesitation whatsoever, depends on a move that makes it all happen in the blink of an eye. And that move is snapping your left hip out of the way.

How Aggressively Do I Snap?

Another issue that you may ask yourself is how aggressively do I snap? This depends on how hard you want to go after the ball. The left hip snap should be at least as aggressive enough to outrace your arms back to impact. After all, THAT is the real name of the game. Obviously, if your arm speed is syrupy and slow, the need to snap your left hip back is lessened to some extent. But if you tend to be a little quick with your hands and arms, even after learning to soften them up a good bit using a hip driven backswing, then you will have to pay some more attention to making sure your left hip gets out of the way that much quicker.

Snapping the left hip back at a 45 degree angle can also allow you to really go after the ball if you want to seek some more distance by letting it all out. Usually, when you try to hit the ball harder to stretch out a drive, for example, the risk is overusing your arms. But give a really aggressive left hip snap a try to hit the ball harder. Hitting the ball harder with your hips can indeed accelerate your arm downswing and create enormously leveraged centrifugal power. The downside, however, is that you clear you left hip out so quick that the arms get left a touch behind, and a push results because your hands did not have enough time at impact to square up the clubhead. But unless you are a touring pro, this is actually pretty hard to do. Sure, Tiger Woods may sometimes get "stuck," but it seldom happens with lesser golfers. Unless you clearly see a pattern emerge of pushes due to failing to close the clubface, outracing your arms to impact by too much rapid hip clearing is just not that much of a problem. An occasionally push is a small price to pay to overcome big slices and duck hooks.

HIP TO HIP FOR BEGINNERS:
SUPER FAST LEARNING YOUR SWING BACKWARDS

If you are a beginning golfer or a high handicapper, you may be much more concerned about simply making some type of impact with the golf ball. The Hip to Hip Method can help you get started hitting pure solid shots from the beginning, if you are willing to spend some time on a drill that can teach you to better learn the golf swing in reverse. You do this by focusing on where you should try to be at impact, and learning to strike the golf ball like a pro does from day one. This drill will guarantee perfectly straight and solid golf shots, even for a beginner.

The Impact Drill

If you as a beginner really want to learn quickly how striking a golf ball solidly feels and you do not want to wait several years to learn it, try the following practice drill. Set up to the golf ball with a 6 or 7 iron, with the golf ball off your left heel. Instead of taking the club back and swing at the ball like you normally do, from a normal address posture, address the ball using what I call the "hips cleared stance." Simply change your address posture so that you straighten your left leg, put most all of your weight on it, and fully turn your hips at address to the "hips cleared position" until you belt buckle faces the target. By doing so, you are essentially at address in the very same position a touring pro's body is in when he or she makes impact with the golf ball. Illustration 4.6 shows how to try this at the practice range to get a feel of what it is like to hit a golf ball with the hips open at impact.

Remember, you are not trying to hit the ball hard with a big swing using this drill. You are only trying to hit straight, solid shots. This "Hips Cleared Stance" position will enable you to do it. So go ahead from this address position and while staying on your left leg with you belt facing the target, simply swing your arms back without getting out of that position—be sure to use NO SHOULDER TURN. You will only be able to swing your arms back to about waist height and not much more. But then go ahead and hit the golf ball. Hit it hard! You will be amazed to discover that you are hitting the golf ball solidly and straight from the very beginning! Due to the frozen state of your legs, hips and shoulders, you will not be able to hit the golf ball very far at all. But you will indeed hit good, strong, solid shots straight down the fairway target line. And you will immediately gain a complete sense of what your arms feel like at impact, and how the golf ball feels properly struck when your hips have fully cleared out of the way.

I strongly recommend that if you are a beginner, or high handicapper, you try hitting a large number of balls at practice initially using the "Hips Cleared Stance." This will enable you to get the feel of actually hitting a golf ball very well from the beginning. This drill will help you learn how critical it is to have the right impact position, and it will prove to you that hip clearance at impact, together with a weighted and straightened left leg, will deliver guaranteed results. You will prove to yourself that you can from the very beginning learn to hit a golf ball solidly. Learning this first is the hardest part. Learning to create some power by making a full backswing is the easy part.

Learning the Golf Swing In Reverse, and Impact Very Quickly

What can we garner from this "Hips Cleared Stance" exercise? The key point is that even a day one beginner can learn to hit a golf ball straight and solidly from this position because it places the arms into the perfect swinging position to deliver the clubhead again and again solidly into the back of the golf ball. This suggests that the very best way to learn the golf swing is in reverse. If you are a beginner, you should use the "hips cleared stance" to learn how to correctly get into the one and only acceptable impact position, using your arms properly back and forth in the impact zone, BEFORE attempting any backswing movement of the hips or shoulders.

Ill. 4.6—Try hitting practice balls using this posture at address and for the entire swing to learn the feeling of having the hips open at impact.

Only after learning how to make impact with the ball should a turn of the hips and the shoulders be incorporated into your swing.

Of course even beginners love to take a powerful cut at the ball, and I fully understand that your patience will be sorely tested if all you do is spend the next year of your life hitting shots by swinging your arms only. I recognize that whatever your level of skill and experience, you are not going to try to make full swings with your arms only but will be using your arms, hips and shoulders. But this is an extremely important learning tool. My very strong recommendation is that whenever you have time to hit a bucket or two of practice balls on the driving range, that you at least hit the first 20 or 30 shots, using a 7 or 8 iron, with the "Hips Cleared Stance." This will reinforce (every time you practice) EXACTLY what correct impact should feel like and where all of the parts of your body need to be at the moment of truth.

So give this routine an earnest and committed try over a 3 to 6 month period, whether you are a beginner, a mid level handicap player or a scratch player needing to get to a better and much more consistent impact position. After hitting 20-30 shots in this manner, go ahead and return to your normal full swing to finish out your practice routine. You will be surprised indeed over a 3 to 6 month period how much of this will begin to sink into your subconscious and you will literally find yourself beginning to take backswings that will lead you into the "hips cleared stance" position at impact. Once you get yourself on this track, your learning curve will accelerate in way you never imagined.

LEARNING HIP TO HIP FROM NOVICE TO EXPERT: WHAT ARE THE SWING SENSATIONS, MILESTONES AND BY PRODUCTS?

Another important aspect of learning the Hip to Hip Method to swing a golf club is what I refer to as "milestones." What are the milestones or markers in terms of swing feeling and sensations you can begin to sense to give you some type of confirmation that you are on the right track? Are there any signposts or milestones in terms of swing sensations you should begin to feel as you improve your ability to make your hips dominate, guide and govern your swing? I believe there are.

The following list of these so called milestones may not be totally applicable to you and are most likely not in any sense exhaustive descriptions of what you may begin to sense as you improve your Hip to Hip performance. But the following summaries of sensations are the ones I have personally encountered as I experienced my hips gaining greater and greater influence over my entire golf swing. These are not sensations to strive for in any conscious sense whatsoever. But they are simply described to help you determine whether you are making progress in letting your hips take their rightful place as the dominant movement in your golf swing. And finally, I end this chapter with a summary of the incredible side benefits to your golf swing I believe you will gain as you place more and more focus on how well your hips are working during your swing.

Pointing with the Right Hip

One of the first sensations you will notice when focusing on starting your swing by drawing your right hip straight back away from the ball or target line is that you will strangely feel as though you are sticking the right side of your rump out in an exaggerated fashion. Are you really doing this? The answer is no, but it sure feels that way. By going from not fully winding your hips during the backswing to cranking them back, you will really start to sense that your right hip really does move out of the way going back. But as you concentrate on drawing the right hip back, the initial sensation of artificially feeling your right butt protrude will eventually fade away as you get better and better with your backswing hip windup.

Pressure on the Right Heel

Another key sensation you should begin to feel as you strive to draw your right hip back to start your backswing is increased pressure on your right heel as your backswing progresses. This is a very good sign. It will mean to you, like it means to Tiger Woods, that you are not swaying your body weight outside of your right foot going back, but are gathering the coil of your hips over your right foot and loading your right side with a rotational wind up and coiling of your hips. This is where your weight should go during your backswing, and moving your weight in this direction will firmly establish your balance during the entire golf swing.

The Downswing Transition and Getting Grounded

As your hips turn better going back, you will want to develop the absolutely essential takeover of your downswing by the lead of your left hip back to the target at the very beginning of the downswing. This is the master transitional move that is a must for you to make the right downswing move back to the ball. How will you know that you are starting to start your downswing with a forceful drive of you left hip? As you keep trying to snap your left hip back at a 45 degree angle to your body, your left hip will slowly but surely begin to take over the transition and downswing. And a feeling or sensation will come with it. What is the sensation? It will begin to occur to you that once in a while, not consistently for sure, but once in a while, you will find yourself making a strangely powerful move back to the ball. And the sensation will be that of actually sensing your hips crank the whole rest of your swing back to the ball with a huge amount of torque.

The sensation will be that your hips crank forcefully back to the ball, and that your torso almost feels as though it is sinking into your feet. This is a sensation that Ben Hogan referred to as "being grounded." What it actually reflects is the strong unwinding motion your legs and buttocks generate as they rotate forcefully against the ground and twist against the ground underneath you. Another related sensation may be an abrupt tightening of your left arm at the beginning of the downswing as the hips twist back to the target and draw the left arm tight, much like the sudden tightening of a lug bolt with wrench. In *Classic Instruction,* Bobby Jones described the transitional unwinding of the hips at the beginning of the downswing as follows: "The hips lead as the unwinding begins, and by pulling against the hands and the weight of the club, draw the left arm taut." Another feeling you may sense is an occasionally noticeable increase in the cocking of your wrists at the start of your downswing.

Posting Up the Left Leg

As your downswing progresses, you may begin to feel your left leg post up by straightening abruptly. This is feedback that your left hip is beginning to snap into place, out of the way in the correct fashion. If there is any doubt that a decisive straightening of the left leg during the downswing is critical to a strong unwinding and clearing of the hits and a good impact, heed the crystal clear advice of Bobby Jones in his book, *Bobby Jones on Golf (Revised Edition).* In it, Jones said, "The left knee must bend to accommodate the turn of the hips and body made in reaching the top of the swing. But from the moment the motion changes direction and starts downward, the left knee begins to straighten. The left leg really must act as a brace against which the player hits. *Under no circumstances must the bend of the left leg be permitted to increase after the downstroke has been started.*"

The Hips Release: The "Flip Over Sensation"

As your ability to pass the club squarely through the impact zone with your hips rather than a heave ho over the top motion or a rolling of your hands and wrists, you will begin to notice, and feel, how decisively and aggressively your hips are beginning to unwind. You will more frequently have the sensation that your hips are spinning so forcefully that they almost "flip over" your left foot and straightened left leg in a rapid circular motion. You will begin to actually feel this sensation, as though you are actually hitting the ball with your hips. There will be no doubt in your mind when this feeling occurs that you cleared your hips about as strongly as possible.

The Magical "Finished Feeling" At Impact

Are there any advanced sensations to let you know that you have mastered the unwinding of your hips and the clearing of your left hip at impact? In fact, there are. Although this sensation is fleeting and I must admit, very difficult of repetition, you may occasionally get the sense that a split second before impact, just before you hit the ball, you have actually "finished" your swing. That is, your sense will be that your hips have completely unwound, you are somehow "floating" over the top of the ball, and that the only thing left to do, which does happen next, is that your arms pass through the impact zone. This is what I call the "magical finished feeling."

This most definitely is not a sensation that can be consciously sought or replicated. However, it is a definite feeling you may experience. But you will experience it only if the clearing of your hips at impact has been total and exhaustive and your timing is impeccable. If and when you manage to pull this sequence of movement off, you will come to understand what it really means to have your hips leading the downswing. You will actually feel what it is like when the hips have done their job ahead of your arms and hands. There is nothing in your swing left at that magical moment except the inevitable clearing of your arms and hands into the back of the ball.

The reason this sensation is fleeting is that it essentially is the feeling that you can get only out of a very rare perfect shot. The feeling exists only with completely perfect timing and sequencing of the hips, shoulders, arms, hands and clubhead. This is the ultimate feeling of the chain reaction described by Ben Hogan. While it is a special moment to hit a pure shot with this sensation, it is not essential to a good round of ball striking. You can play very well for weeks, months or even a year or so at a time without ever having this particular sensation. But if and when you do, you will know that on that particular swing, your hips were working as well as they possibly can.

The Soft Hands at Impact

Once again, the goal of the Hip to Hip Method is to get to impact using your hips to square the clubface into the ball rather than rolling your hands over to do it. Therefore, it should come as no surprise that one of the sensations you may encounter at impact is a feeling that your hands are actually soft and relaxed as the club smashes into the back of the ball. This "soft hands" feeling will again demonstrate to you that your wrists are not rolling over to square up the clubhead.

Too Much Mastery of Hip to Hip: Am I Getting "Stuck?"

Assuming you get to the level of unwind and clearing your hips in a manner that unquestionably is leading your arms and hands into the ball at impact, you may be wondering, can I overdo this hip turning and unwinding? The answer is definitely yes, but very unlikely. It is indeed possible to unwind your hips during the downswing so fast that your arms do not catch up at impact, which leaves the clubface open to most likely cause a push of the shot to the right. Some refer to this as "getting stuck."

Unless you never hit a hook shot, ever, or unless you are plagued by a long term unresolved problem pushing the ball, my strong recommendation would be to forget about getting stuck. Why? In my experience, very, very few players ever have enough of an athletic burst of energy to unleash their hips quite so fast at impact. Getting stuck is generally only a problem for top touring pros. It is true that Tiger Woods expresses worry from time to time about getting stuck, but who among the rest of us mortals on earth unwind their hips as unbelievably quick as Tiger?

Hip to Hip and Prevention of Swaying

As you learn to use your hips more effectively using the Hip to Hip techniques described in this book, you will begin to notice that a lot of other swing problems seem to correct themselves almost by themselves. Many of these problems solved result from a correct use of the hips. One of the key benefits to turning your hips correctly in a Hip to Hip manner is the elimination of swaying and laterally sliding "off the ball."

A big problem for many golfers is the inability to keep their upper body stable during the backswing and not sway laterally away from the target. But this problem goes away when the right hip is drawn straight back during the backswing with your weight shifting back as well onto your right heel because this creates a rotational winding of your torso rather than any swaying away from the target. You are much, much more easily able to play with your body weight never straying beyond the insoles of your feet because your hips compel your body torso and weight to turn instead of slide.

Likewise on the downswing, by shifting from a draw of the right hip back to a snap of the left hip 45 degrees to your left while straightening your left leg, your hips shift to your left foot but not beyond. You prevent yourself from sliding laterally toward the target and coming off the ball as the hips rapidly rotate back to the target and then to the left of the target line as the left hip rotates out of the way and clears, leaving a clear and unimpeded route at the impact zone for the arms and hands to pass. If swaying or coming off of the ball has been a problem for you, these problems will disappear as you learn to incorporate the Hip to Hip Method.

Hips and Balance

Another critical area where the Hip to Hip Method works well is in the maintenance of your dynamic balance throughout the entire swing. The hips and your waist serve as the center of gravity of your golf swing, and once the hips begin to rotate properly back and forth, leading the shoulders and arms and hands throughout the swing, you will notice that any real balance problems will disappear.

You will find yourself not falling over the ball toward the target line with your right foot as you follow through. You will have your left foot totally grounded and solidly anchored to the ground during impact and follow through, and you will find yourself beginning to finish your swing with almost all of your weight on your straight left leg at the finish, totally in balance. The hips are the foundation of excellent balance, and by moving your hips in the right directions using the Hip to Hip Method, your balance will once and for all be established securely during your entire golf swing.

THE CRITICAL IMPORTANCE OF STAYING DOWN AND THROUGH THE BALL

When learning to forcefully unwind your left hip during the downswing using the 45 degree hip snap technique, you must be keenly aware how tempting it becomes to "come out of the shot." Coming out of the shot means that as you are approaching impact, not only your hips unwind, but also your upper torso unwinds improperly. The improper unwinding of your upper torso results from your turn of your upper torso toward the target during the downswing, coupled with a lunging forward and lifting of your upper torso so that you do the very opposite of staying "down and through" the shot.

Coming off of a shot is very harmful to your swing health. It can result in your clubhead not quite getting down to the ball, meaning that you can hit a shot thin, very thin, or even top the ball as you lift up with your upper body at impact, drawing your swing arc inches above the very back of the golf ball. Coming off of the shot can also cause you to leave the clubhead open at impact, resulting in a push or slice.

To avoid this coming off of the shot, you must learn to stay "down and through" the shot. This means that as your left hip aggressively turns out of the way at impact, you must nonetheless stay down with the ball and avoid starting your follow through until your have hit your shot. How do you do this while spinning your left hip so aggressively out of the way in clearing the impact zone? You accomplish it by "covering the ball." Covering the ball means that as your left hip clears out of the way at the impact zone, your upper body and torso remain steady over the ball. You do not begin your follow through until you have completed impact and hit the golf ball.

Staying down and through the ball is obviously easy to say, but how can you insure yourself that you can do better and better in staying down with your shot? I recommend a drill that will train you to stay down with the shot while nonetheless clearing your left hip aggressively at impact. The fun thing about this drill is that you do not have to have a golf club in your hands to perfect "covering the ball" nor do you have to hit a lot of practice balls to ingrain it into your repertoire.

The drill is simply an isometric that works, pure and simple. When you are taking a shower in the morning, simply stand and turn your hips into the impact zone, opening your left hip to the target and straightening your left leg. As you are standing in the impact position in the shower, simply let your arms hang down toward the imaginary ball, and lean over toward the ball. You will feel a definite stretching of your left lateral back muscles as you stand in this arched position.

Continue to hold this isometric position for 60 to 90 seconds at a time, stretching your left side as your hold your upper torso over the ball while your left hip is completely turned toward the target. Several days of doing this isometric exercise will do wonders in helping you stay down and through the shot at impact as you master your hip unwinding during your downswing. Covering the ball is an essential fundamental in hitting a golf ball, and it is fully compatible with the Hip to Hip Method of swing a golf club. But failing to stay down and through the ball is as fatal as not using your hips properly. So use this isometric religiously to stay down and through your shots.

USING THE HIPS TO PROMOTE TEMPO

Using the Hip to Hip Method to improve your mechanical technique in swinging the golf club creates a large number of swing improvement benefits—a better swing plane, a better foundation of balance, a stronger coil of the hips and shoulders, and better insurance that the left hip will lead the rest of the downswing and clear out of the way while your arms pass through the impact zone. But another important benefit of Hip to Hip is the role it can play in developing and maintaining good swing tempo.

Swing tempo is one of the hardest parts of the golf swing to learn and once learned, it seems impossible to maintain. Even the very best players have to struggle with their tempo. Tempo tends to fluctuate, often widely, from day to day. But good tempo is as critical and important as the mechanical aspects of swinging a golf club.

Entire instructional books are devoted to establishing good tempo. Each player has to find his or her best swing tempo suited to his or her temperament and personal ability. Excellent golfers can swing quick or slow, but must within their own swing speed keep a good tempo. So how can you do it better?

Some players focus on swinging smooth or slow, and some focus on a slow and deliberate takeaway. What is the ideal tempo? Under the Hip to Hip Method, any swing speed, slow or quick, will work. A slower swinging player will have an elapsed swing time from takeaway to impact of anywhere from 1.5 to 1.8 seconds. A faster swinging player may have an elapsed swing time of .75 to 1.25 seconds. But it is not the total swing time that necessarily matters. The key is that, whatever the player's actual swing speed happens to be, he or she does not allow the arms to outrace the hips going back or coming through the impact zone.

If tempo is judged on that basis, then the Hip to Hip Method should help promote good swing tempo. Your backswing is not begun by a jerk of the club away from the ball by the hands and arms, which is a leading cause of getting "too quick." Instead your backswing is begun by a rotation or drawing back of your right hip, which almost more than ½ of the way to the top of your backswing, involves no arm or hand motion at all. Instead, the club is taken away from the ball in a much more smoother motion by which the arms and hands are passively being pulled away from the ball by the winding of your right hip and corresponding winding of your shoulders, which in turn pulls your right hand away from the ball. The hips start the swing out in front of your shoulders and arms, and set a foundation of excellent tempo for the rest of the swing's duration whereby the hips are not overcome by the arms. Your tempo sequence is . . . . draw the right hip . . . . finish winding the shoulders . . . . , and SNAP! The hips start out in front and stay out in front.

HIPS AND POWER: THE HARDER THE BETTER

Okay, you may be thinking to yourself, this Hip to Hip Method sounds fine and dandy, but it seems to be all about squaring the clubface. What you may really be asking yourself is where can I learn more about power? In my view, if you want to pour on more power, work on rotating your hips harder through impact. If you try to pound the ball with your hands or arms, you will end up coming over the ball or rolling your wrists and hooking. But as Hogan correctly claimed, the hips on the downswing cannot go too fast. And the faster they unwind the more room you will have to pick up your arm speed automatically and within the lead of the hips. So the more power you want, the harder you should snap your hips back to the ball coming through.

Chapter 5

FULLY TURNING YOUR SHOULDERS: SWING TECHNIQUE OR CONDITIONING?

I have set the following discussion about shoulder turn under the Hip to Hip Method apart in a separate chapter because it raises a critical issue about how to make a full turn in a golf swing. Obviously, due to the skeletal connection, a larger hip turn will promote a larger shoulder turn. We all strive to make a full turn on the backswing. But will simply trying to turn do the job?

For youngsters and scratch golfers in their teens and twenties, the answer is probably closer to yes. These gifted species are often known to the rest of the golfing world as "limberback." The level of their natural flexibility is simply amazing. To a younger golfer with a supple physique and lots of muscle flexibility, it is not much of a feat to be able to wind up the shoulders easily 90 degrees if not even more. Some young power players can wind up their shoulder 100 to 110 degrees at the top of their backswings.

For golfers who are in their 30's or older, and particularly middle aged and senior golfers the answer is a clear no. If you are not a limberback, this is a very important point. Swing technique alone will not achieve a full shoulder turn, and trying to make a full backswing shoulder turn will do more harm than good. Forcing yourself to wind your shoulders takes too much physical effort that can seriously divert your mental focus by trying too hard to attain the impossible. Trying to wind up the shoulder too much can also easily deteriorate into moving or swaying off the ball going back, or worse, fooling yourself that a lifting of the club with overly vigorous arm action is actually a bigger shoulder turn.

If you are not a limberback, then the solution to creating and keeping a full shoulder turn is enhanced flexibility. I have a few isometric exercises that will definitely help. Do all three of these stretching exercises at least once a week, whether or not you play or practice, and always do them as a part of your practice or play warm up. They only take a few minutes, but the dividends in terms of a fuller shoulder turn will be rich.

The Shoulder/Hip Flexibility Drill

This drill is tough to achieve right off the bat, and if you have any type of back problem, this drill may prove too much of a strain. But if you really want a top shoulder turn and you are lacking in the muscle flexibility you once had, give this a try.

Take a golf club, and hook it across your back with the insides of your elbows. Then, taking a normal address position, practice turning your left shoulder under your chin really full and deep. Try to wind your left elbow under your chin down enough that it can touch your left knee. Do this back and forth, winding and unwinding about 10-20 times. Then take one big last wind up. Refer to Illustration 5.1 for an example of how to try this exercise. This time take your left elbow and lock it on the inside of you left thigh, keeping your balance. You will feel a tremendous stretching of your right leg and hip as you hold this isometric position for about 1 minute. This will take some real work in the beginning, but keep at it until you can at least somewhat comfortably lock in that left elbow against the inside your left leg.

The Shoulder Turn Drill

After completing the first shoulder flexibility drill, do the next one. Here, you will stand at address, but hold the golf club

Ill. 5.1—The Shoulder/Hip Flexibility Drill

in your left hand only. Take your right arm and wrap it under your left elbow while cupping your right hand over your left shoulder. This places your right arm in the position of being like a claw grabbing your left shoulder. Then make your backswing, but as you near the top of your swing, take the claw grip in your right hand over your left shoulder and give it a huge crank, and pull your left shoulder under and around your chin as far as you possibly can. Hold this isometric position for 60 to 90 seconds. See Illustration 5.2 to see how to try this drill.

The Rotator Cuff Stretch Drill

This final drill not only enhances your shoulder flexibility, but also provides you with some additional protection against shoulder injury during your swing by minimizing the risk of rotator cuff problems. Simply take a club, holding the clubhead in your right hand and lay the club grip first over your left shoulder and across your back. Then take your left hand, reach behind your back, and grab the grip of the club at the top of the grip. Next take your right hand and try to work it along the grip of the club along the grip toward the left hand, and try to pull your left hand as close to your right hand as possible. This will pull and stretch your left shoulder extensively. Hold this isometric position for 60 to 90 seconds. See Illustration 5.3 for an example of this drill.

I promise you that if you want to build in some more shoulder turn flexibility, the above isometric drills will help you tremendously. This will free you from having to force a shoulder turn. These drills will greatly help you make a shoulder turn that is as natural as possible, and more dependent on flexibility and hip rotation than forced shoulder turning.

*Right
Hand
Pulls*

*Stretch
Left
Shoulder*

Ill. 5.2—The Shoulder Turn Drill

Ill. 5.3—The Rotator Cuff Stretch Drill

CHAPTER 6

USING YOUR HIPS TO CONTROL SWING PLANE

For years, golf instructors have focused heavily on the proper swing plane. What is swing plane and what should your swing plane look like? Usually teachers use the term swing plane in referring to the imaginary line at the top of the swing running from the left hand through the left arm and shoulder to the golf ball. Ben Hogan used the concept of an imaginary plane of glass resting on top of the golfer's shoulders and angled to the ball as an observer would see, standing behind the golf ball and the player, and looking down the target line. If the hands at the top of the swing were higher than the plane of glass, the golfer's swing would be viewed as being an upright swing, and if the golfer's hands at the top of the swing were below the pane of glass, the swing would be characterized as a flat swing plane.

For years, instructors have focused heavily upon swing plane and debated whether an upright or flat swing works better. Most everyone agrees that swing plane is an individualized trait, and that a player adopts whatever swing plane style works best for the particular player. Flat plane swingers and teaching advocates stress keeping the right elbow tucked closely into the side of the player's body and a low takeaway to promote swinging the shaft and clubhead more around the body, which in turn results in the clubhead being delivered into the back of the ball on a relatively shallow angle of impact.

The most famous practitioner of the flat swing plane was Ben Hogan. Sequence photographs of his swing show his left hand and arm at the top of his backswing on a plane below his right shoulder so that his swing pattern more closely resemble a merry go round rather than a Ferris wheel. Other successful flat plane swingers include John Mahaffey, Lee Trevino, Gary Player, and Bobby Jones.

Of course, looks can be deceiving, and Hogan's arm swing plane, which did appear to become more and more flat over time, was not as flat as many writers and instructors have suggested, for two reasons. First, Hogan's posture at address evolved over his career from a more or less bent over spine angle into a more erect, stand up position. Consequently, Hogan's shoulders did turn on a more horizontal plane than normal. While this in turn flattened the appearance of his arm swing as compared to other players, it did not flatten Hogan's arm swing relative to his angle of body and hip rotation caused by his erect spine angle.

Second, although Hogan's swing later in his career seemed more flat, his backswing had in fact shortened to the point that his clubshaft never reached parallel at the top of his backswing. This three quarter length swing prevented his arms from fully swinging up to a more upright position. Compared on an apples to apples basis with other players, Hogan's swing would have appeared to be quite a bit more upright in the later stages of his career had he swung the clubshaft fully to the top to a parallel position.

Upright swing plane advocates stress taking the club back on a much steeper angle at takeaway so that at the top of the swing, the left hand and arm are at an angle to the ball whereby the left arm is above the right shoulder between the right shoulder and the player's head. The most famous example of using an upright plane successfully has been Jack Nicklaus and his fabled "flying elbow." Commentators and instructors frequently noted that during Nicklaus's backswing, his right elbow did not stay tucked in close or glued to his body at the top of his backswing, but moved noticeably away from his side as his arms swung up high to the top in a vertical fashion more like a Ferris wheel than a merry go round. Other top players with upright swings have included John Daly, Scott Hoch, and Fred Couples. Perhaps the most extreme upright swing is Jim Furyck's, whose arms at the top of his swing are so steeply pitched and vertical that his left hand is almost over the top of his head at the top of his backswing.

Should you adopt a swing plane that is more flat or more upright? I think a good case can be made that you have a unique individualized swing plane that will work for you, but it is not a question of style as to which method you adopt. Instead, your swing plane should be exactly the arm swing plane governed and controlled by the turning of your hips and shoulders during the backswing with your arms and hands following their lead. The winding of your hips and completion of your shoulder turn will swing your arms and hands automatically along a backswing pathway that will be natural and unembellished. No extra moves to work your arms and hands into the right backswing plane are needed at all.

Your arm plane at the top of your swing, if you have a somewhat normal build and average height (using regular length shafts), will be somewhere along the line of your left arm in a line right across your right shoulder, or a perhaps a smidgen above it—not too steep and not too flat. Your arms should not initiate or control the backswing, but should during takeaway and the entire backswing, be relaxed and simply follow the lead of the right hip going back. You can then trust your hips and shoulders to work your arms, hands and golf club into the proper swing plane, eliminating another set of instructional complexities you should not have to worry about. Golf is difficult enough without having to worry about swing plane as if it were a separate discipline!

CHAPTER 7

HIP TO HIP DRILLS AND
EXERCISES FOR RAPID LEARNING

It is indeed true that on "paper" as described in this book, the Hip to Hip Method sounds simple enough. But I again caution you that it is not. Although one of the key purposes of this book has been to help you conceptualize your golf swing in a manner that will simplify the learning process, there is much athletic work to be done. Grasping and embracing a golf swing concept as an intellectual matter is not enough to build the improvements into your swing that I hope this book will provide. Before you can mold your golf swing into a reliable athletic machine, you must learn the moves of your hips under the Hip to Hip Method as muscle memory. Only when you have built the moves outlined in this book to strengthen the swing domination of your hips to the point of being able to automatically trust your muscle memory, have you truly "learned" the Hip to Hip Method.

The purpose of this chapter is to provide you with a number of isometric exercises and drills. These isometric exercises and drills, if practiced with some routine regularity and self discipline, will significantly shorten your learning curve and speed up your rate of golf swing improvement. I have also included several drills that may help you overcome a few particularly egregious fundamental golf swing flaws that, if they plague you, must be ironed out of your swing before you can effectively incorporate the principles that are a part of the Hip to Hip Method. For those of you who are firmly committed to some really intensive speed learning, the isometric drills, practiced daily for a period of 30 or so straight days can lead to permanent and dramatic swing improvements.

STRETCHING AND WARM UP EXERCISES

The following drills are helpful to help you warm up prior to a round. These are particularly good if you are a middle aged or senior golfer. If you wish to avoid using these drills on the practice tee at the golf course, try them at home before you get there. You will like the warm up benefits of using these drills.

The Shoulder/Hip Drills

In chapter 5, I discussed the use of several shoulder turn and hip stretching drills to improve the turning movement of your shoulders during the backswing. Again, these drills were The Shoulder/Hip Stretch Drill, The Shoulder Turn Drill and the Rotator Cuff Stretch Drill. While these drills are excellent techniques you can use over time to improve your shoulder turn, I remind you that these three isometrics work wonders as a several minute warm up routine prior to your round.

The Arm and Shoulders Stretch Drill

This is another good warm up drill. Simply take a longer club such as a driver or three iron, grip one end with your left hand and one end with your right hand, and lift the club over your head as if your were lifting a barbell. Then push the overhead club as far back over and behind your head as possible. Hold it for 30 seconds, rest about 30 seconds and do the stretch again another 30 or so seconds. This will stretch out the front of your chest and shoulder muscles and help relax your arms at address.

STAYING DOWN WITH THE BALL DRILL

As I indicated in Chapter 4, it is critically important to swing your arms through the impact zone with your left hip completely cleared out of the way. This requires an aggressive, and rapid rotation of your hips back to and past the target line. But a focus on simply clearing your hips is not enough. The hips must be cleared fully at impact WHILE YOU AND YOUR UPPER BODY OR TORSO SIMULTANEOUSLY STAY DOWN AND THROUGH THE BALL.

The problem with learning a strong downswing hip unwinding and clearing is that it invites you, or worse, even causes you to come out of the shot at impact and off the ball. To combat this tendency while learning a stronger hip unwinding during the downswing, you must also learn to stay down and through the ball while unleashing those hips. But the other problem is that your downswing happens so unbelievably fast that you cannot effectively learn to stay down and through the ball by consciously practicing it on the driving range.

My recommendation is that, in lieu of trying to consciously practice on the driving range, you learn how to stay down and through the ball with an isometric exercise. I call it the Staying Down with the Ball Drill. You can do this isometric exercise in a 60 second time span. I suggest you stand in front of a mirror to do this at first so that you can actually see what covering the ball looks like, at least in an exaggerated manner.

Simply face the mirror as if you were addressing the ball, and put yourself in the impact position. While facing the mirror, turn you hips toward "the target" so that they are fully cleared out of the way, straighten your left and put virtually all of your weight on your left leg. While standing on your left leg with your belt buckle fully facing your imaginary target, look down to where your ball would be if you were actually going to hit a shot. Then with your chest facing the mirror, try to bend your torso over and forward toward the ball. The more bend the better. You will feel a definite stretching of your lateral muscle on the left side of your back. This is the muscle that needs to be stretched out some so that your torso stays down over the ball, hovering over it almost like a hummingbird, while your hips clear out of the way. Refer to Illustrations 7.1 and 7.2 for examples of the Staying Down with the Ball Drill.

The Staying Down with the Ball Drill is an extreme position and you will undoubtedly feel a major stretch that may take a few days of soreness to work through, but you can be fully assured that in front of the mirror, at least, you are without question covering the ball and learning fully what covering the ball means. Over a several week period, if you do this isometric once a day, you will realize HUGE improvement in your ability to stay down and through your shots. It is my belief that under the Hip to Hip Method, mastering your ability to stay down and throught the ball at impact is one of the most important fundamental improvements you can make.

Another time saver way to use the Staying Down with the Ball Drill is to try it while you shower in the morning. Simply stand on your left leg with your hips fully open to "the target" and grasp your right knee with both of your hands. This will be a daily powerful reminder to you and your subconscious that staying down at impact by covering the ball as your hips clear out of the way is the correct place to be at impact. I can assure you the learning you will obtain by consistently doing this drill will carry into your golf swing without any further conscious effort on the course or the driving range. But the dividends you will reap from covering the ball will be truly significant and almost immediate!

MASTERING SWING BALANCE:
THE FEET TOGETHER DRILL

The Hip to Hip Method will over time actually promote good balance throughout your golf swing. But you may find yourself in the position of losing your balance so much that you need some additional and quick help. If your balance is poor,

Ill. 7.1—The Staying Down With the Ball Drill

Ill. 7.2—Staying Down With the Ball Drill

there is little point in learning much else about how to swing a golf club. You must have good balance first before learning any other swing skills. Here's how to get it and get it quickly.

You could be losing balance by falling back on your right foot on your downswing, or finding your right leg and foot coming off the ground at impact and swing out away from your stance during the follow through. Or you could be sliding your hips toward the target with bent knees at impact so that you almost fall forward in your follow through. If you are losing balance in your golf swing for any of these reasons, try hitting 40 or 50 balls on the driving range each practice session, using a 5 or 6 iron, and keeping both of your feet dead together against each other. This is obviously the most narrow stance possible with which you can swing a golf club. You will find it very difficult if not impossible to overswing the club with your arms and hands while keeping your balance. You will be able to swing about 75% as fast and hard as you normally do. But this training drill will do wonders in teaching yourself how to keep your balance all the way through your swing.

This drill in my opinion is completely foolproof and it will result after a few practice sessions in your creation of complete balance. If you cannot hit solid, straight practice shots using the feet together stance, keep trying. It will eventually work and your lack of any sense of balance will vanish. Once your are comfortable hitting solid straight shots with your feet together, and finishing with almost all of your weight on your left foot, go back to your normal stance and enjoy your new rock solid balance!

DEFEATING OVER THE TOP:
THE RIGHT HAND PRACTICE DRILL

One of the most perplexing problems faced for the most part by middle and higher handicap golfers is coming over the top on the downswing. You find yourself taking the club back, then the right hand overtakes the rest of your swing and it throws the arc of the club outside the in to out arc of the clubhead into the back of the ball and instead the clubhead is delivered into the ball from outside the target line. This produces moderate to severe pulls if you somehow manage to square the clubface up with the outside in path the clubhead is traveling, or moderate to severe slices if in addition to coming into the ball from outside the target line, the clubface stays open. If you have this problem, you may want to try the right hand practice drill.

To work on this drill simply hit the first 30-40 shots of your practice sessions with your right hand only. Start slowly, and even extremely slowly to gain the feel you need to deliver the clubhead into the back of the ball. At first swing a golf club with your right hand only and hitting a golf ball will seem completely impossible. But over a few practice sessions, you will begin to see how your right hand and arm swing can effectively deliver the club correctly to the back of the ball, and will experience solid straight shots. Once you return to swinging with both hands, your first several shots will feel weird and you can expect a topped shot or two. But after a few swings, your regular swing will return but with a better understanding of your right arm swinging along the target line instead of over the top.

The right hand practice drill is also effective for you if you are a low handicapper seeking to improve your tempo. The right hand drill forces you to turn your hips back to the target before your right arm swings through the impact zone, and makes you wait on the ball. It is impossible to release your right arm and hand into the ball swinging one handed unless your hips have cleared out at impact. Returning to your normal swing, you will find that your timing, sequence of motion and overall tempo have improved after 30-40 right hand only shots.

DOWNSWING HIP ROTATION DRILLS

Another set of drills to help you initiate your downswing using the lead of your hips focus on hip rotation or unwinding to the target. Try these and use the one or two drills that work for you.

The Washing Machine Drill

This drill is designed to get your hips leading the rest of your swing back to the target the instant you reach the top of your backswing. Take a club and hold it in front of you with your hands hanging in front on your hips in the middle of your body, and the club held perpendicular to your body or parallel to the ground. Then in a totally relaxed and loose fashion, standing straight up, simply rotate your hips and upper body as if you were the spindle in the middle of a washing machine clockwise in a rotating motion similar to your backswing.

As you turn back as far as you can without any forced motion, your arms and hands will be carried along by the inertia of your body rotation. As you reach the "top" of your swing, which is actually just a rotation of your hands around your waist, initiate a decisive, but unhurried unwinding of your left hip back counter clockwise to what would be your target area if you were making an actual golf swing, and turn your entire upper body torso and hips to the target.

As you complete this unwinding, start another "backswing" windup by re-rotating your hips and upper body clockwise back in a backswing type fashion. At all time during this process, keep your arms, shoulders and hands totally relaxed. As you turn back and forth, you will begin to feel your arms continuing to wind up as if you are making a backswing while your left hip is already spinning back toward the target line. The action is very similar to the winding and wrenching you see when you open the top of a washing machine and see the clothes spinning in a circular fashion in one direction while the spindle in the middle is spinning in the opposite direction, creating a torque effect on the clothes.

This washing machine effect is exactly the type of torque action that is created when, during an actual golf swing, your hips decisively lead your swing back to the golf ball as your arms and hands reach the top of your backswing, with the result that your wrist cock actually increases at the beginning of the downswing! This is not something you should ever try on the driving range or golf course during an actual swing to hit a golf ball. But the drill, which does not require anything but a room, and a club (no ball, no driving range, no course), will greatly strengthen your ability to make the transition from your backswing to your downswing with a decisive, leading and forceful unwinding of your left hip back to the ball and target.

The Hip Spin Drill

This is probably the best drill you can do to get your hips moving first during the downswing. You do not have to actually be hitting practice balls to use this drill so you can do this at home in the morning or evening. Take a club and hook it across your back at your waist level using the insides of both your elbows to hold the club in place. Stand as if you were addressing a ball, with the posture you would use. Then, simply rotate your hips back and forth as if you were actually swinging a club back and forth. See Illustration 7.3 for an example of how to use this drill. Focus on decisively initiating your downswing with a powerful turn of your left hip back to the target, finishing on a straight left leg with all of your weight onto your left foot at the finish. Or focus on snapping your left hip at a 45 degree angle back toward the target from the top of your backswing. But don't stop at the finish but move immediately back into a windup of your hips as you would do if you were making an actual backswing. Draw your right hip back good and deep, or feel your belly button winding up over your right heel.

Ill. 7.3–The Hip Spin Drill

Do this repeatedly, back and forth 15 to 20 times. If you next hit actual practice balls on the driving range, you will notice a difference. The drill is also a good quick solution if you are hitting practice balls or playing and find yourself hooking the ball. Chances are that you are getting your hands back to the impact zone quicker than your hips and rolling your wrists over to close the clubface. Try this hip drill 20 or so times and see if your hook does not abate somewhat if not fully once your hips get back to impact first.

The Downswing Only Drill

This drill is very easy, but a great way to encourage your hips to lead your downswing. Take the first 30 to 40 balls on the driving range, and with a 6 or 7 iron, take your backswing and stop. Fully wind up your hips and your shoulders and hold your arms in a limp fashion so that your clubshaft is loosely resting across the top of your shoulders. The key here is to totally remove any arm action from your position at the top of your swing.

From there, after pausing at the top for several seconds, mentally checking that you have made a complete hip and shoulder turn backswing, simply unwind your left hip as aggressively as possible back to the target. I do not mean a casual unwinding, but a forceful, decisive turn of the left hip back out of the way. You will be surprised to learn that your limp arms are somehow miraculously flung back to the ball and you will actually begin to hit solid golf shots using this hips only downswing.

By winding up fully with your hips and shoulders at the top of your backswing with your clubshaft resting on your shoulders and your arms as loose as dish rags, the full emphasis you place on very aggressively unwinding your left hip back to the target will begin to ingrain itself into your normal swing after hitting 30-40 practice shots in this fashion. This exaggerated hips first downswing move should significantly boost your ability to start the downswing with your hips rather than your arms. Try this wonderful drill in a 3 to 5 day a week practice range routine for about a month and see how much better your hip action becomes as an automatic first downswing move!

ACKNOWLEDGEMENTS

I want to thank my wife, Maggie Elliott for the love and support she gave me while I wrote this book. Her patience with me at home with the word processor was remarkable. Thanks to my son, Will Elliott for inspiring me to take the game of golf back up; I am so proud of you and all that you do. I also want to thank my own swing coach, Lew Ferrell of Charlotte, North Carolina. Lew helped me think better about how to make a stronger move in clearing my hips better at impact. Lew also understands the need for balance in a golf swing and the importance of staying down and through the shot. He also got me to recognize the importance of maintaining muscle flexibility in the golf swing. I also want to express my deep appreciation to my good friends, Weldon Wyatt and Tom Wyatt of *Sage Valley Golf Club* in Aiken, South Carolina. It has been a great privledge and pleasure over the past few years to be a member of *Sage Valley*, which is a golf course and club membership that is one of the finest in the world. Weldon and Tom have made their vision become reality, and have made a truly historical contribution to the game of golf. I am very grateful for their friendship and look forward to many years of great golf and wonderful company at the one place in the world where golf is played "as it should be".